West Side Story

West Side Story

Barry Monush

AN IMPRINT OF HAL LEONARD CORPORATION

Published in 2010 by Limelight Editions
An Imprint of Hal Leonard Corporation
7777 West Bluemound Road
Milwaukee, WI 53213

Trade Book Division Editorial Offices
33 Plymouth St., Montclair, NJ 07042

Printed in the United States of America

Book design by Mark Lerner

Library of Congress Cataloging-in-Publication Data is available upon request.

ISBN 978-0-87910-378-1

www.limelighteditions.com

For Michelle,
who first brought Tony and Maria into my consciousness,
with much affection

CONTENTS

PREFACE

As a lifelong movie aficionado I've explored many eras and genres, but the sixties still give me the greatest pleasure, just as there's nothing I enjoy more than musicals. And since in that particular decade the Best Picture Oscar was presented to no fewer than *four* musicals, it's easy to see why it speaks (or perhaps sings?) to me.

One of those Best Picture winners was *West Side Story*, and like all ten honorees in the Academy Awards' top category from 1960 through 1969, it is an all-time favorite film of mine. Ask me to see it again minutes after I've just watched it, and I will gladly say yes. In fact, I had the opportunity to see it on the big screen (at Manhattan's Ziegfeld Theatre) while writing this book and had no qualms about revisiting it, despite having just run through the DVD in order to take copious notes. It is *that* sublime to me, *that* electric an experience, *that* meaningful in my life.

As I sat doing research at the Lincoln Center library, I couldn't help but think of how some of the movie I was writing about was actually filmed on that very spot. And despite everything that great arts complex has given New York, a small, nostalgic part of me wished those streets and buildings that had served such a pivotal role in making this motion picture were still there, so that I might walk through them, spotting familiar backdrops against which the "Prologue" unfolded, vicariously reliving key moments. But time marches, or dances, on. . . .

When I was approached to contribute to Applause Books' *Music on Film* series, the title that came instantly to mind was *West Side Story*. I knew it would be fun and interesting to write about, that my enthusiasm would be sincere. So I jumped at the chance to celebrate something that deserves to be celebrated, despite the efforts of select people throughout the years to downplay or dismiss this superb contribution to the motion picture art and popular culture.

So I thank John Cerullo for the chance to do so; Tom Lynch for sharing my passion; Lori Lynch for her musical expertise; and Bernadette Malavarca for assisting me in putting this book together.

Right, daddy-o . . . so let's rumble. . . .

INTRODUCTION: CONTINUING STORY

When the mere act of someone repeatedly snapping their fingers can bring to mind a specific work of art, then it is safe to say that work of art is seminal. Catch someone doing just that (snap . . . pause . . . snap . . . pause . . .), and there is little doubt that a wide margin of people will instantly think of *West Side Story*. There is also the possibility that the notes Leonard Bernstein wrote to accompany the snapping (a motif that makes up a portion of the musical's "The Jet Song")—an E natural that jumps an octave to the high E natural, then descends to C sharp and then to A before hitting the dissonant E flat, which is held for another two and a half measures—will run through everyone's mind. *West Side Story* might also be the first dramatic work conjured up at the mention of "gangs," or may well epitomize what constitutes dancing in terms of storytelling. The word "rumble" is synonymous with the musical because of its big set piece, the tragic confrontation between the warring Jets and Sharks. There is no denying *West Side Story* is a point of reference that has been ingrained deeply in our cultural mind-set for more than five decades.

Unlike certain works that make a major impact in their day and then fade away for all but the most heavily versed in entertainment lore, *West Side Story* remains high profile, potent, and important. Pop culture reminds us of this. Just in recent years, Bart Simpson enacted its final scene in *The Simpsons* episode "Bart Gets Hit by a Car"; in *The Sopranos*, Tony (James Gandolfini) commented on how one is best advised to "stick to your own kind" regarding his mistress, a choice of words equated with the musical by his bemused therapist, Dr. Melfi (Lorraine Bracco); Jack Nicholson made a tense Adam Sandler sing one of the show's myriad hit numbers, "I Feel Pretty," in *Anger Management*; when Will Ferrell and his colleagues confronted a staff of rival newsmen in *Anchorman*, the scene deliberately paralleled the musical's famous rumble; in the Broadway show *Urinetown*, the song "Snuff That Girl" featured the company cavorting in finger-snapping gang patterns that aped Jerome Robbins' fabled choreography, much to the delight of savvy audiences; on *House M.D.*, Hugh Laurie snidely called a cop "Krupke," while on *Curb Your Enthusiasm*, Larry David could not get over the fact that he had encountered a policeman who bore that same name. Although the original stage musical contained all of the elements mentioned above, the fact remains that the majority of people (those doing the spoofing or paying tribute and those watching) did not first experience the material in person but became aware of it because of their exposure to the 1961 movie adaptation.

One result of creating a motion picture from an already established source is that it prompts certain viewers to seek out the original, which is not always to the benefit of the film. Plenty of plays, short stories, articles, and books have been badly distorted, inadequately realized, or misguidedly revamped in the not-always smooth transition to celluloid. Experiencing how something was originally intended by its creators can cause a turn of opinion on something heretofore beloved. But that does not appear to be the norm for this work. Certainly the film of *West Side Story* has its detractors (several people involved with the original stage version among them), but most audiences embrace it to such a degree that even seeing its live incarnation cannot live up to the cinematic experience. Its place in the pantheon of theater is high, but its place in movie history is just as high, and might be much higher.

It is not a motion picture of which people have a neutral opinion. It does not simply exist, as certain movies do, to be glimpsed casually, off-handedly, and then promptly forgotten because it is just one of so many of a similar ilk. It is unique, hard to forget or mistake for something else; it never seems to lose its freshness, never threatens to wither away into irrelevance because of changes in behavior and audience expectations or the inevitable passage of time. It is the sort of movie experience that is so all encompassing, so emotionally charged, so visually dazzling, so larger than life that it seems about to burst out of the confines of the screen, certainly out of a television screen or video monitor, where most of us have been obliged to watch it in recent years. Of course *everything* intended for a movie theater should be seen there, given the chance, but *West Side Story* is one of the hallowed few films that even people who wouldn't think of plunking down money to see in a movie theater what they've already seen for free (or perhaps even own a copy of) have no qualms about tracking down in order to get that added jolt of witnessing it on the big screen. And the bigger the screen, the better.

It is no secret to even the most marginally movie trivia-aware that *West Side Story* looms large in the motion picture landscape and always has. It was the top 1961 release at the box office and swept the Academy Awards, bringing home a total of ten, coming in second place for the record after *Ben-Hur*'s eleven trophies, won two years prior. The soundtrack album, despite containing mostly voices of unbilled "ghost" singers, was no less a sensation, becoming the longest charting LP of the decade and still holding the spot of longest charting number 1 album *ever*.

Quality, of course, is a factor in its stature. But it is not a given that something outstanding elicits a wide and fervid following; we've all seen plenty of wonderful films that have never made so much as a tiny scratch on the public consciousness. Certainly the brilliance of how music, drama, and dance were seamlessly and thrillingly blended is an essential reason *West Side Story* endures and towers above most other pictures from its genre, and from its era. But I believe another key element in the gut reaction it receives from those who "get it" has a great deal to do with its source material, William Shakespeare's *Romeo and Juliet*. Although your average inexperienced student (or adult for that matter) has been known to cringe at the mere mention of the Bard's name, this is the one play of his whose premise is ingrained in our minds from a pretty early age and that draws a deep emotional response, just because of what it is about, even before we've read a word of it. Despite being written in the sixteenth century, Shakespeare's tragedy hits a nerve in each generation and has stayed relevant and timeless: it addresses intolerance, the purity of young love in an imperfect world, parental pressures and adults' inability or refusal to understand the mind-set and needs of teenagers. The idea of adapting its story line and themes to a modern setting was a master stroke (of course Cole Porter had already modernized Shakespeare with *Kiss Me Kate*, which had its origins in *The Taming of the Shrew*, but that, being a comedy, did not elicit the same visceral response from audiences). The connection to *Romeo* instantly gave the work a certain degree of respectability, which was only enhanced by how well it was executed.

But *West Side Story*'s following would be small and cultish if the film only achieved respectability within the cultured crowd who seek high art. The fact that it is driven by youth, involves street gangs and hip lingo, and radiates a degree of "coolness" (it even contains a song called "Cool"), an element missing from the musical genre in the eyes of select parties, has made it resonate with the working class and the provincial, with the average audience who has no interest whatsoever in high art. It has crossed boundaries in ways that too few musicals have.

At the time *West Side Story* premiered on Broadway, two of its four central creators, choreographer-director Jerome Robbins and composer Leonard Bernstein, already had very high profiles in their fields and were even familiar names beyond that. Librettist Arthur Laurents was an admired dramatist but wasn't in a position to accrue a following in the way these two men had. As fortune would have it, the fourth name, the least known at the time, lyricist Stephen Sondheim, would garner a devotion that in many ways surpassed the adulation accorded both Bernstein and Robbins. The intense interest in the output of each collaborator further expanded the amount of attention and degree of examination given their piece for generations to come.

Without the exemplary contributions of each of these men, there would be nothing to admire and continually celebrate onscreen. Although it is nearly impossible to imagine *West Side Story* without the soaring sounds and melodic excitement Bernstein brought to it, the tightly plotted book Laurents wrote, or the Sondheim lyrics that have become ingrained so thoroughly in the minds of so many, the piece was first and foremost, as so many involved were quick to point out, the brainchild of Jerome Robbins. As original stage and film cast member Tony Mordente bluntly put it in the documentary *West Side Stories*, "Anybody has any questions about who was the genius behind all of this—Jerry Robbins is the man behind the gun. I mean . . . he put the bullets in, he cocked it; he shot it. And everybody else was smoke and noise."

West Side Story

CHAPTER 1

Backstory

Jerome Robbins

Jerome Robbins no doubt got pretty tired of telling the story of how, in 1947, an unspecified actor friend came to him troubled over how to relate to the character of Romeo, as he was scheduled to do a scene from the Shakespeare play as part of his acting class. This caused Robbins to consider how one might approach the role from a contemporary perspective, how to interpret Romeo in today's terms. From there Robbins began formulating in his mind a modern-day Romeo and Juliet story, told in song and dance.

Some have speculated that the unnamed actor in question was Montgomery Clift, who was involved romantically with Robbins during that time, though this has been refuted or dismissed for lack of evidence. The anecdote always gave the origins of *West Side Story* an interesting quirky twist, however: imagine that one of the great modern actors of the postwar years, someone in no way associated with the musical genre, might have been the catalyst of what would become one of the genre's great achievements. In any case, Robbins clearly wanted certain details left vague in his oft-repeated tale, to the degree that when he was being interviewed on the religious program *Look Up and Live*, shortly after *West Side Story*'s debut on Broadway, he dropped any mention of an outside source, instead telling the host it all came from a time Robbins himself sat down to read the script of *Romeo and Juliet.*

At the time the *Romeo* idea began germinating in his head Jerome Robbins was at the top of his game, having become one of the most in-demand names in the world of choreography, for both ballet and Broadway. He had entered the world as Jerome Rabinowitz on October 11, 1918, in New York City, but was not raised in the metropolis that would become the backdrop for his most famous work; he grew up across the river in Weehawken, New Jersey. Unlike most masters of his craft, he did not start learning to dance as a small child. He was already well into his teens when his older sister suggested he join her at the Dance Center in New York. There he studied under Gluck Sandor. In the summers he joined the creative team at the Tamiment summer resort in the Pocono Mountains, where he danced in shows and occasionally staged numbers.

This led to his first contact with Broadway, dancing in the ensemble of a "play with music" (the latter by Frederick Loewe of future Lerner and Loewe fame), *Great Lady*. It opened on December 1, 1938, and closed after a 20-performance run. Nevertheless, Robbins was back on the boards twice during the following year. The first show, *Stars in Your Eyes*, spotlighted Ethel Merman and Jimmy Durante, with a score by Arthur Schwartz and Dorothy Field. The company included Mildred Natwick, Richard Carlson, Tamara Toumanova, Dan Dailey, Nora Kaye, Clinton Sundberg, Mary Wickes, and, billed as one of the "Gentlemen of the Ballet," Robbins. It chalked up 127 performances at the Majestic Theatre, closing in time for Robbins to return to his summer camp duties. This led directly to *The Straw Hat Revue,* conceived and staged by Max Liebman to showcase the young talent from Tamiment, among them Danny Kaye, Alfred Drake, and Imogene Coca. It would run for 75 performances at the Ambassador Theatre during the fall of 1939.

The following year Robbins made the decision to join the newly created Ballet Theatre, the first large-scale American company of its kind. He worked with them extensively over the next several years, including on a tour of Mexico. This trip over the border brought about Robbins' very first (and often forgotten) motion picture credit, providing some of the choreography for a 1943 film called *Yo bailé con Don Porfirio* (which translated into *I Danced with Don Porfirio*). As much as Robbins enjoyed performing, he was more excited by the prospect of creating dances and began formulating a piece about three sailors on leave in New York, something that he hoped would reflect the current state of the country in the midst of World War II. By doing so, he felt he could also remove any suggestion of stuffiness that had made some audiences steer clear of the art, having his dancers behave and look like real people would, albeit real people with superb terpsichorean skills. Looking for a new score to accompany his dance, he turned to Leonard Bernstein, who was on the brink of his own breakthrough.

Leonard Bernstein

Leonard Bernstein entered the world seven weeks before Robbins did, as Louis Bernstein, born on August 25 in Lawrence, Massachusetts. Although his father had no doubt that his son would join the family cosmetics business, young Leonard or Lenny (as he was called by everyone, despite the name on his birth certificate) was far too obsessed with music to heed his parent's command. He began studying piano at ten; at age twelve he entered the New England Conservatory of Music. By fourteen he was heard performing light classical pieces on the radio. His fascination with music was all encompassing; once he had mastered the piano he ventured into both conducting and composing with equal commitment, studying the former at the Curtis Institute of Music in Philadelphia. In 1940 he became a part of the Boston Symphony Orchestra's summer institute, Tanglewood, where he was already gaining a reputation for the passionate and flamboyant manner in which he conducted, successfully conveying his own excitement for the composition to the audience. He was mentored by Serge Koussevitzky, for whom he became assistant conductor.

Around the time he was first approached by Robbins to score his ballet, Bernstein was invited by Artur Rodzinsky to be assistant conductor for the New York Philharmonic, an impressive accomplishment for someone who was all of twenty-five years old. But things got even more impressive when Bernstein was obliged to fill in for an ailing Bruno Walther on November 13, 1943, a seminal moment in twentieth-century music history. So astounded was the audience by Bernstein's brilliance that day that his triumph was reported on the front pages of both *The New York Times* and *The Herald Tribune*. He was the youngest person to ever conduct a Philharmonic concert.

His overnight fame was such that he could have easily turned down Robbins' request to work on his ballet project, but Bernstein was not the sort to opt for a light workload and plunged into the assignment, providing the choreographer with just the sound he was looking for. Their collaboration, entitled *Fancy Free* and featuring Robbins himself as one of the sailors, debuted as part of the Ballet Theatre's program at the Metropolitan Opera House on April 18, 1944, to rapturous reviews that applauded Robbins for bringing a fresh and bracingly exciting perspective to ballet. Bernstein's score had blended jazz and classical in a brassy exuberance that suggested his talents did not lie exclusively in conducting.

It was the production's set designer, Oliver Smith (who would later play a part in the success of *West Side Story*), who first suggested they turn the idea into a full-scale Broadway musical. Once again taking the topicality of a nation at war into consideration, Robbins and Bernstein aimed to get their revision up and running as soon as possible. Rather than simply expanding what he had already written, Bernstein came up with an entirely new score. Chosen to pen the lyrics were two entertainers/writers with whom Bernstein had worked on summer camp shows, Betty Comden and Adolph Green, who would also fill two of the leading roles. Feeling inexperienced in structuring a Broadway musical comedy, Robbins fell back on veteran George Abbott to do the directing, sticking expressly to the choreography. The choreography, however, was a crucial element to the piece rather than something reserved for select numbers; there was a constant impression of a moving, swirling ensemble, feelings and emotions of the characters expressed through dance.

In the newly revamped *On the Town*, Robbins had already shown that he could bring his ballet sensibility alive in the traditional "musical comedy" format. Opening on December 24, 1944, at the Adelphi Theatre, with Oliver Smith serving as both the production designer and the producer, *On the Town* was yet another testament to the unlimited talents of Robbins and Bernstein. They had captured both the anxiety and the joy of life in wartime, making this a seminal contribution to musical theater. Bernstein's rhythms were soaring, plaintive, melodic, often thrillingly discordant and original in their sound. The songs could easily qualify as "show tunes," but there was something richer, more classically exciting about them that deserved to be given a closer hearing. Together, Bernstein, Comden, and Green came up with one song that would even be adapted as an unofficial anthem for the city, "New York, New York" ("a helluva a town" . . . or "a wonderful town," for those who became familiar with it by way of MGM's heavily revised 1949 movie adaptation). The show settled in for a 462-performance run and would eventually transcend its dismissal by certain factions who considered it expressly and specifically "of its time," taking its place as one of the key works of Broadway musical history.

Robbins and Bernstein had conquered Broadway and could have easily made that their preferred place of expression, in tandem or otherwise, had they both not been so keen to keep creating elsewhere. There was also the feeling in their respective fields that the traditional musical format was "slumming" for artists of their caliber and that working on Broadway only would prevent them from being taking seriously. This most certainly nagged at Bernstein, who was guilted by his mentor, Koussevitzky, into returning to the classical world as soon as possible. His stature there continued to rise, as reflected in his appointment (on his twenty-seventh birthday) as conductor of the City Symphony of the New York City Center of Music and Drama, succeeding Leopold Stokowski. When next he teamed with Robbins it was back in the world of ballet, composing music for *Facsimile* in 1946.

Robbins was less concerned than Bernstein with precisely *where* his creative juices were allowed to flow and returned to Broadway within a year of *On the Town*'s opening with *Billion Dollar Baby*, working once again with Oliver Smith as production designer and for the first time with costume designer Irene Sharaff, who would become another member of the *West Side Story* team on both stage and screen.

Robbins' follow-up show, *High Button Shoes* (1947), brought him his first Tony Award, the standout number being a knockabout chase that incorporated the feel of a Mack Sennett silent movie farce, thereby proving that the choreographer could pull off something that was great fun as well as artistic. Staying in a more comical mode, *Look Ma, I'm Dancin'!* (1948) was important for being the first time Robbins received credit as the actual director, though he shared the task with George Abbott. When this particular musical was being put together, Robbins first approached Arthur Laurents, whom he had known for several years but with whom he had not yet collaborated professionally, to write the book. Although Laurents turned down the offer, he was an admirer of the musical genre and very interested in working with Robbins.

Arthur Laurents

Like Robbins and Bernstein, Arthur Laurents was born in 1918, the eldest of the trio, his birthday a few weeks before Bernstein's, on July 14. He knew at an early age that he wanted to be a writer and took a New York University course in writing for the radio. His instructor was a director-producer for CBS; this allowed him the opportunity to submit a script of his own that impressed the right parties enough to be produced on the air, with Shirley Booth in the lead. Laurents soon became gainfully employed in the medium until his busy schedule was interrupted by war service. His experiences there inspired him to write a play, *Home of the Brave*, which dealt with anti-Semitism within a small unit on duty in the jungle. Favorably reviewed, Laurents was hailed as a new writer of merit; among the many moved by the play was Leonard Bernstein. The box office results were serviceable, not sensational, and the play closed after a sixty-nine-performance run. It did, however, bring Laurents a movie sale (the 1949 independently produced adaptation admirably addressed prejudice at a time when Hollywood customarily steered clear of such topics, but changed the focus by making the target of racism a black man instead of a Jew). His next effort, *Heartsong*, closed out of town, but did bring an offer to go west and work in the movies, at Metro-Goldwyn-Mayer. Laurents and Hollywood, however, were a bad mix. He was therefore willing to fit something more to his liking into his schedule when Jerome Robbins made him an offer to collaborate on a musical.

Once Robbins had the idea in his head for the *Romeo* project, he immediately thought of Bernstein for the music and then wondered if perhaps Laurents might be the right man to do the book. The three met in New York in 1949 to discuss the direction they should take. As Robbins initially conceived it, the musical update would involve the conflict between Irish Catholics and Jews on Manhattan's Lower East Side during the Easter-Passover season, therefore addressing anti-Semitism as *Home of the Brave* had. Bernstein and Laurents were certainly intrigued by the possibilities, but Laurents made clear that he did not want to be involved if it was to be an opera, which Robbins and Bernstein were seriously considering. Taking a cue from its initial setting, they began referring to the project as *East Side Story*.

Because Laurents was still employed back in California and Bernstein's duties as conductor kept him either in New York or hopping about the globe, guest conducting elsewhere, the two men realized they would have to work separately as they pieced together the preliminary ideas. They soon concurred that this method of collaboration was counterproductive, and they weren't all that excited at the prospect of developing something that bore an uncomfortable resemblance in its plotline to the 1920s Broadway favorite *Abie's Irish Rose*, in which a Jewish boy falls in love with and marries an Irish Catholic girl, much to the displeasure of their families. In a short time they admitted defeat and went on to other projects, as did Robbins. It would be another six years before *Romeo* was up and running for real.

In the interim Laurents found himself blacklisted and Robbins naming names, an uncomfortable situation that brought tension to their friendship, though Laurents did not hold such a grudge that he would not work with the choreographer. Bernstein finally earned another Broadway credit, providing both music and lyrics to a 1950 version of *Peter Pan*, starring Jean Arthur and Boris Karloff. Ironically, only three years later, Robbins would choreograph another adaptation of the James M. Barrie tale that surpassed and pretty much obscured the earlier attempt in popularity, collaborating again with Adolph Green and Betty Comden, who came in to work on some of the lyrics. Laurents was called on to help doctor a revue show starring Bette Davis that Robbins was directing, *Two's Company*. Robbins did his own doctoring on another Bernstein–Comden–Green credit, *Wonderful Town*, which proved to be one of the big successes of the 1952–53 Broadway season. That same season saw Laurents' longest running effort to date, *The Time of the Cuckoo*, starring Shirley Booth, who brought home a Tony Award for her performance. During this time the fourth name in the *West Side Story* collaboration was doing his best to establish himself.

Stephen Sondheim

Twelve years the junior of his three collaborators, Stephen Sondheim was born and raised in Manhattan, but it was his family's summer residence in Bucks County that brought him into contact with lyricist Oscar Hammerstein II. Becoming very close to Hammerstein and his family, Sondheim would show his junior efforts at musical composition to his famous mentor. During his school years at Williams College, he studied music under Milton Babbitt and wrote a musical adaptation of *Beggar on Horseback* called *All That Glitters.* After graduation, his first serious attempt at writing a score, *Climb High*, went unproduced. Rather than launching his career on Broadway as he hoped, his entry into professional show business came about through television, where he worked as a writer on CBS's adaptation of *Topper.*

Through a contact with producer Lemuel Ayres, Sondheim got the opportunity to write the music and lyrics for an adaptation of a play by twin brothers Julius and Philip Epstein (of *Casablanca* fame), *Front Porch in Flatbush.* The novice songwriter eagerly dove into the project (called *Saturday Night*) and half the money was raised for the production, but Ayres died and left Sondheim high and dry; there would be no major New York production of this work until 2000. Sondheim, however, had the material ready to go for an audition piece, which came in handy when Martin Gabel decided he wanted to adapt a James M. Cain novel, *Serenade*, into a stage musical. Gabel dangled the idea in front of Bernstein and Laurents, who in turn hoped to get Robbins involved.

Robbins preferred they pick up on their *Romeo* project, so Bernstein soon bailed out. Searching for someone else to write the music, Gabel had Sondheim play his *Saturday Night* score for Laurents, who wasn't too enthusiastic about the music but highly impressed by the cleverness of the lyrics. The project came to naught, but Laurents and Sondheim had at least made contact. When wheels finally got spinning on the *Romeo* musical, it happened not in the shadow of Broadway but out on the West Coast.

CHAPTER 2

Broadway Story

August 25, 1955, was Leonard Bernstein's thirty-seventh birthday; it was also, according to his recollection, the date on which he and Arthur Laurents once again crossed paths, at the Beverly Hills Hotel. Bernstein was in town to conduct at the Hollywood Bowl, while Laurents had been summoned by MGM to work on the screenplay for a planned remake of *The Painted Veil* (Laurents backed out of the project, which ended up as *The Seventh Sin*, with Karl Tunberg the credited writer). The two men discussed their regret that nothing had ever come of the *Romeo* project, and when they brought up recent articles in the *Los Angeles Times* about rising tensions between Chicanos and Caucasians in local neighborhoods, suddenly Laurents wondered if perhaps *that* was the angle to go with. But Laurents didn't feel comfortable writing about a city and a people that were not part of his consciousness and suggested they relocate the story back east, with gang wars between Puerto Ricans and whites on Manhattan's West Side. Suddenly everything started to click and Robbins, when contacted, showed equal excitement at this approach. Further discussions ensued after Robbins arrived on the Coast to stage the "Small House of Uncle Thomas" number for Fox's film of *The King and I*, the first time he would work on an American motion picture. There had been previous attempts to get him into this field, first an offer from Paramount to adapt *Look Ma, I'm Dancin'!* into a showcase for Fred Astaire and Betty Hutton (the film the two performers ultimately starred in together, *Let's Dance*, had nothing whatsoever to do with this property). During the 1950s, the same studio dangled the possibility of a contract in front of the choreographer, but he was far too busy with ballet and Broadway and was not eager to be tied down to any such agreement.

Initially the idea was for Bernstein to provide both the music and the lyrics for the *Romeo* project, but he worried about his conducting workload interfering with that much responsibility and suggested that his previous collaborators, Betty Comden and Adolph Green, be brought in to give him a hand. The lyricists had other commitments, besides which Laurents did not feel that their smart, sophisticated way with words was suitable for something he hoped would have a grittier feel to it. Bernstein was still hoping to share the task with someone else. Laurents ended up solving that problem when he ran into Stephen Sondheim at a party. Sondheim inquired about the long-dormant *Romeo* project and Laurents suddenly realized this could be the aspiring songwriter's chance to make the leap to Broadway. Sondheim, however, was none too overjoyed by the offer, as he wanted desperately to make his mark writing both lyrics *and* music, and wasn't quick to say yes. His mentor, Oscar Hammerstein II, thought otherwise, feeling that it would be a grievous mistake for Sondheim to pass up an opportunity to work with such revered artists as Bernstein and Robbins and encouraging him to accept. Reluctantly Sondheim agreed to audition his *Saturday Night* score for Bernstein, who was immediately pleased with what he heard and consented to their collaborating. From late 1955 into early 1956 they worked on the songs, until Bernstein put things on hold when the opportunity arose for him to get another project off the planning board and onto the Broadway stage, his adaptation of Voltaire's *Candide*. Likewise, Laurents took advantage of the lull in the *Romeo* schedule to finish up a play, *A Clearing in the Woods*. Robbins had a firm offer to choreograph and direct a show that Comden and Green had created for their former nightclub partner Judy Holliday, *Bells Are Ringing*.

West Side Story, as Robbins and his team were now referring to the gestating musical, would have to wait, yet again.

In his "News and Gossip of the Rialto" column in the January 22, 1956, issue of *The New York Times*, Lewes Funke reported "That Leonard Bernstein–Arthur Laurents–Steve Sondheim musical, *West Side Story*, is finished," then went on to inform readers that they would have to wait until the following theater season to see it, because of the aforementioned previous commitments and because the search for unknowns to carry the show would be a long and painstaking one. The *Times* was certainly jumping the gun, as the show was unlikely at that point in time "finished" to the degree that the article suggested.

The 1956–57 theater season saw *Bells Are Ringing* opening on November 29 at the Shubert Theatre to enthusiastic notices and tremendous box office, making it one of the major hits of the day. (It would run for 924 performances, bringing Tony Awards to Holliday and her costar, Sydney Chaplin.) Two days later *Candide* arrived at the Martin Beck to far less critical excitement; this famously cynical piece struggled to find an appreciative audience. January 10 marked the premiere of *A Clearing in the Woods* at the Belasco; it closed a month later and seven days after Bernstein's musical shuttered. Although *Candide* would grow in stature over the years because the score featured some of the composer's most outstanding themes, Bernstein took the failure hard. He was now more eager than ever to move on to the *West Side Story* project, in hopes that it would put him back in the good graces of the Broadway community. In the spring of 1956, Cheryl Crawford and Roger L. Stevens signed on as producers.

Laurents' book had ingeniously updated all of the pivotal characters and elements of *Romeo and Juliet*, so that it was quite clear to the well-versed just what *West Side Story* was based on. "Fair Verona" was now New York's West Side tenements; the warring Montagues and Capulets became the Jets, the Caucasian gang, and the Sharks, their Puerto Rican rivals; Romeo and Juliet became Anglo Tony and Puerto Rican Maria; Paris, the man to whom Juliet is betrothed much to her displeasure, became gang member Chino; Juliet's protective cousin, Tybalt, who ends up slain by her lover, was now her brother, Bernardo, the head of the Sharks; Romeo's best friend, Mercutio, was Riff, the Jets' leader. Anita, Bernardo's girlfriend and Maria's confidante and fellow shop worker, would fill in for the Nurse and bring an important missive to Maria's lover, paralleling a similar scene in Shakespeare when the hapless lady is taunted by the Montague clan; Romeo's trusted Friar Laurence was replaced by Doc, the owner of the drugstore at which Tony was employed. The disapproving Prince was Lieutenant Schrank. The Capulet social gathering crashed by Romeo and his cohorts at which he first lays eyes on Juliet was turned into a dance at a gymnasium; the play's most famous, quoted, and parodied scene, the "Wherefore art thou, Romeo?" exchange of devotion between the young lovers at the balcony to Juliet's room, was relocated to a fire escape. Whereas Shakespeare had depended upon a plague to prevent the important news of Juliet's "faked death" reaching Romeo, Laurents wrote a strong scene of further unwarranted racism that causes an angered and humiliated Anita to lie and tell her tormentors that Maria has been killed by Chino, thereby prompting the tragic denouement. Shakespeare had Romeo kill Paris in Juliet's tomb before taking his own life in grief, thereby prompting Juliet to join her lover in death; things would play out much differently in the update, with Chino gunning down Tony and Maria renouncing the gangs for all the pain their hatred has caused, rather than choosing to kill herself.

The heroine would remain alive at the climax, but Laurents had written a show in which two of the main characters, Riff and Bernardo, would end up dead on the floor of the stage as Act I came to an end, while the hero, Tony, would join them at the finale. Clearly *West Side Story* was not going to be your average "musical comedy" and therefore was something of a hard sell—so hard that once Cheryl Crawford realized she would be producing something that was financially risky and a bit of a downer, she began to have doubts, making suggestions to the team of creators to "lighten" things up and not chance alienating the sort of people who customarily paid for tickets on Broadway. Of course anybody getting wind of the fact that this was a modernized *Romeo and Juliet* had every reason to suspect that something unhappy was going to happen by the time the final curtain rang down. Nevertheless, by the spring of 1957, Crawford ended her participation in the show, and Robbins and company had to find another producer to fill her spot.

Sondheim had been friends since the late 1940s with Harold Prince, who had made the leap into producing in partnership with the older Robert E. Griffith, with a pair of back-to-back musical hits written by Richard Adler and Jerry Ross, *The Pajama Game* and *Damn Yankees*. At the time the two men were offered *West Side Story* they were working out of town on a musical version of *Anna Christie* called *New Girl in Town*. After seeing what Laurents and Sondheim had come up with, Prince and Griffith were very excited by the prospect of handling something that would not be a traditional evening of song and dance and agreed to come on board. Between them they managed to raise the $300,000 required.

Not concerned with casting established names, Robbins took great care in finding the right people to fill not just the principal roles but even the smallest of parts. For once the dancers were not to be treated as background figures to toss off an occasional number, but would be actual characters. It was more customary to treat dancers and singers as separate parts of the ensemble; Robbins would be breaking that tradition by finding performers who could, hopefully, dance, sing, and act equally well. "We tried nearly all the young actors you see in television shows about juvenile delinquency," Robbins told *The New York Times*. "But generally they lacked the kinetic physical energy, the ability to move, that dancers have."

Larry Kert auditioned for the show with the hope of perhaps landing the part of Riff, only to end up with the coveted lead. Born (in 1930, as Frederick Lawrence Kert) and raised in Los Angeles, he had done some extra work in films (his sister, Anita Ellis, had done dubbing on several occasions for Rita Hayworth and Vera-Ellen) before heading east to study acting with Sanford Meisner and singing under Keith Davis. Joining a singing and dancing act called Bill Norvas and the Upstarts led to his first Broadway show, appearing with them in the revue *Tickets, Please!*, which had a seven-month run during 1950. Staying in the chorus, he was in another successful revue, *John Murray Anderson's Almanac*, in 1953, and was a cast replacement in the Sammy Davis Jr. musical *Mr. Wonderful*, which included Chita Rivera among its principals.

Dolores Conchita Figuero del Rivero was born in Washington, D.C. on January 23, 1933, the daughter of a musician who had performed both with the Harry James orchestra and for the Broadway musical *Lady Be Good*. As Conchita del Rivero, she won a scholarship to George Balanchine's School of American Ballet in New York, studying under the ballet master. This led to her first contact with Jerome Robbins, joining the company of the touring production of Irving Berlin's *Call Me Madam*, which he choreographed. Her Broadway bow came when she replaced future *Oliver!* choreographer Onna White in the chorus of *Guys and Dolls*, and then danced in the original production of Cole Porter's *Can-Can*. Simplifying her name to Chita Rivera, she appeared in four sketches in Ben Bagley's 1955 off-Broadway *Shoestring Revue* (other newcomers in the cast included Beatrice Arthur and Arte Johnson), which brought her first notice by reviewers. During the run of the show she was lured away to play one of the prostitutes in what turned out to be an unsuccessful attempt to make *Seventh Heaven* into a musical. Peter Gennaro served as the official choreographer, although Robbins came in to help the troubled show at one point. Rivera was certainly in demand, next landing a supporting part in *Mr. Wonderful* and shortly after its closing becoming Eartha Kitt's standby in the short-lived adaptation of *Shinbone Alley*. The role of Anita in *West Side Story* was about to turn her into one of the most exciting talents on Broadway.

Playing the role of Rivera's lover, Bernardo, was a dancer who was actually under the impression that his performing days were over at the time of his casting. Ken Le Roy was the son of vaudevillians and therefore had been ushered into show business at a very early age, making his Broadway debut at eleven in the massive ensemble of Kaufman and Hart's patriotic spectacle *The American Way* in 1939. Later he danced in several seminal musicals of the time, including *Oklahoma!, Carousel, Brigadoon*, and *Call Me Madam*, the last for Jerome Robbins. By the mid-1950s, his ambition was to move over to directing; he thereby hoped to work expressly as an assistant stage manager. So dissatisfied was Robbins was so many of the applicants at the *West Side Story* auditions that he asked Le Roy to read, which led to him becoming the Sharks' leader.

After his first auditions, Mickey Calin (born Martin Calinieff in 1935) was pretty much told he stood no chance of making it into the company of *West Side Story*. He therefore returned to the chorus of the tour of *The Boy Friend*, only to be summoned back for another try. He had already appeared in Sandy Wilson's send-up of twenties musicals on Broadway and been part of the ensemble of the flop revue *Catch a Star!* (among the contributors to this show were Neil

Simon, Lee Adams, and Jerry Bock) in September 1955. Calin was doing stock work in Valley Forge, Pennsylvania when he was told he had not only won a part in *West Side Story* but would have the standout role of Riff.

Carol Lawrence was born Carol Laraia in Melrose Park, Illinois in 1934. Having studied dance as a child, she joined the Chicago Opera Guild Ballet before earning a scholarship to Northwestern University. She journeyed east to look for work, ending up a performer at Leon and Eddie's nightclub before being cast as one of Broadway's *New Faces of 1952*, alongside such other hopefuls as Eartha Kitt, Paul Lynde, Ronny Graham, and Alice Ghostley. The revue was popular enough to run nearly a year and to be adapted by Twentieth Century-Fox into a CinemaScope motion picture, in which Lawrence made her screen debut in 1954. Despite this, jobs were not plentiful in Manhattan, so she went back home, where she found more gainful employment on some local Chicago television variety shows. Returning to New York, she appeared in a run of musicals, starting with *Plain and Fancy*, the City Center version of *South Pacific* (as Liat), the quick flop *Shangri-La* (which boasted costumes by Irene Sharaff, who would work on *West Side Story*), and yet another revue, *Ziegfeld Follies of 1957*. When she came to the audition for *West Side Story* Lawrence deliberately made herself up to look as Hispanic as possible but was sent home by Robbins, who insisted he was looking for someone far less self-conscious. Just being herself, Lawrence possessed the right degree of innocence and had both the pipes to sing the role as well as the necessary dancing experience. The lead was hers.

Among those in the company were Marilyn Cooper (as Rosalia, joining Anita in "America"), who would go on to win the 1981 Tony Award for her featured role in *Woman of the Year*; Martin Charnin (Big Deal), the future Tony Award-winning lyricist of *Annie*; Grover Dale (Snowboy), who would later dance alongside George Chakiris in the French musical *The Young Girls of Rochefort*; and Jaime Sanchez (Chino), who would play Rod Steiger's doomed shop assistant in *The Pawnbroker* (Landau-Ungar, 1965) and the youngest member of *The Wild Bunch* (WB-7 Arts, 1969). There was also a lady playing one of the Sharks' girls who brazenly carried the name Elizabeth Taylor, no doubt leading to a few puzzled *Playbill* readers in the audience. Interestingly, Sanchez was the only company member cast as a Puerto Rican who actually hailed directly from that country.

With *Gangway!* now being given to the press as the name of the show, Robbins insisted on an unprecedented eight-week rehearsal period for the cast, a grueling but ultimately exhilarating experience. The choreographer was known in the business for his demanding personality, his insistence on perfection, and his frequent temperamental outbursts that would often cross the line between disciplinary and downright rude. To instill a sense of "tension" and palpable "competition" between the designated gangs of the story, he insisted his cast keep separate camps during the rehearsal process. The performers couldn't help but admire his determination and insistence on nothing less than their absolute best. Condemnations of his behavior were almost always followed by words of awe at what he achieved, whatever the price.

Despite the fact that the finished work would carry Robbins' very distinctive stamp, he gave a good deal of the Sharks choreography over to his assistant, Peter Gennaro, who came up with many of the steps on "America" and the mambo movements done by the Sharks and their girls during "Dance at the Gym." Robbins, however, had made it clear that any credit for the movement and direction of *West Side Story* would be exclusively his and had had Gennaro sign an agreement up front with the understanding that his contributions would be minimized. In fact, Robbins insisted on the billing "Conceived, Directed and Choreographed by Jerome Robbins," a choice of words that rankled Bernstein and Laurents, who had been the two who had hit upon the Puerto Rican–Caucasian tension on which the whole piece spun.

Robbins and his team had made clear that what they were creating was a stylized piece of theater (or a "poetic fantasy," as they preferred to call it), not a starkly realistic statement about the dangerous escalation in gang violence that was permeating urban centers or *the* final word on racism, although one of the great strengths of the piece would indeed be its potent condemnation of bigotry. Laurents concocted his own bits of gangland slang for the occasion ("frabba-jaba" for incessant chatter, "glory osky" as a version of "oh, my god!") and managed to insert a few startling words like "bastard" and "sperm" at a time when this was not common language in musical theater. Stephen Sondheim's lyrics, however, were obliged to draw the line, with "The Jet Song" opting for "when the *spit* hits the fan" rather than the commonly used excremental expletive. The same song climaxed with the Jets declaring their domination of the "whole *buggin'*, ever lovin' street" which no doubt was a replacement for the four-letter word to end them all. This desire to give the piece a feeling of youthful immediacy while adhering to a lower-class lingo made Sondheim feel uncomfortable about some of the softer lyrics Bernstein had come up with, which made some of the characters sound more "sophisticated" than they would obviously speak, given their upbringing. As the lyrics have become a part of musical theater lore, it is difficult for the many admirers of the work to accept criticism of this discrepancy: the dialogue has come to represent part of the very nature of these characters.

So well, however, was the collaboration clicking that there were few drastic alterations on the road to Broadway. One noticeable change was removing "One Hand, One Heart" from the fabled balcony scene, simply because it was too plaintive and gentle, when the scene required something more passionate to make it soar. A portion of the "Quintet" sung prior to the Rumble was therefore expanded to fill the space, and the final result, "Tonight," became the declaration of Tony and Maria's love as they clandestinely meet on the fire escape, in many ways the most iconic match of song and scene in the whole work.

Bernstein intended the show to conclude with an aria sung by a grieving Maria in response to Tony's death. In writing the script Laurents penned what he described as "dummy lyrics" to convey the moment, assuming that Sondheim or Bernstein would fill in whatever they had in mind. Instead, Bernstein could not come up with anything to his satisfaction and it was agreed that Maria's big speech, admonishing the Sharks and Jets for the awful price paid for their intolerance, was potent enough without conveying it in song.

Much was written in reviews about how "short" Laurents' book was compared to most librettos in musical theater; the author allowed dialogue scenes to be scrapped to make way for songs as Bernstein and Sondheim became inspired by lines he had written. There was also the understanding from the start that Robbins would fall back on dance whenever possible to get the feelings of the characters across, to express the emotions in the story. According to a June 16, 1957, report in *The New York Times*, as the production was progressing, "*Gangway!* promises to be the 'dancingest' show in years, the dancing being, besides intricate and elaborate, most intimately woven with the telling of the story."

To this end *West Side Story* would open with a nearly wordless depiction of the animosity between the Puerto Rican and Caucasian gangs, a combination of balletic grace and teen angst, outbursts of tension blended with stylized action that spelled out the warring nature of the Sharks and the Jets. It was clearly a risky way to begin, asking the audience to plunge themselves instantly into the incongruous combination of gang violence and dance, but it was one reason the reaction was so enthusiastic, as audiences felt certain they were witnessing something innovative and daring.

It was decided that *Gangway!* gave the wrong impression that what they were presenting was more lighthearted than it actually was, so *West Side Story* was reinstated as the official title prior to the out-of-town tryout in Washington, D.C. scheduled to launch on August 19, 1957. The creators would later state that this was a rare instance of a show opening out of town looking pretty much the same way it would appear on Broadway, so few were the eventual changes. At one point they considered putting in another song, "Kid Stuff," but decided that it was too comical for the tone; it was never even heard by an audience.

West Side Story opened at Washington's National Theatre for a three-week run. The press reception was glowing, but whatever words of praise it received were restricted to the three creators who were already known, Robbins, Bernstein, and Laurents. In a gesture of generosity not often found in show business circles, Bernstein felt that sharing credits on the lyrics with Sondheim was not doing the latter any favors and thereby insisted that his own name be removed, allowing the *Playbill* to read "Lyrics by Stephen Sondheim" only. Although there remained contributions by Bernstein that Sondheim was none too eager to call his own, all future sources would cite only him as the lyricist.

The show next moved on to a similar reception at Philadelphia's Erlanger Theatre, and it was obvious that something very exciting was about to happen on Broadway. With a top price of $7.50, *West Side Story* at long last arrived in New York at the Winter Garden Theatre on September 26, 1957, the first notable new offering of the 1957–58 season. (Interestingly, one of the productions that had played at the same theater during the previous season was the Old Vic

Company's presentation of *Romeo and Juliet*, in repertory.) Playing at nearby houses at the time of the premiere were such holdovers from prior seasons as *My Fairy Lady* (at the Mark Hellinger), *Li'l Abner* (at the St. James), Robbins' own *Bells Are Ringing* (the Shubert), and *Damn Yankees* (Adelphi) in its final weeks.

In light of its stylization and compared to the sort of raw material that would come to Broadway in later years, it is almost startling to see how "shocked" certain reviewers were at the content and the subject matter of the show, championing Robbins and his team for executing something with such masterful precision but expressing concern that audiences might be unnerved by gang violence, flashing switchblades, racial epithets, and three principals slain by the evening's end. There was no getting around the fact, however, that this was a major artistic triumph that had accomplished everything it set out to do in blending dance with story, reimaging Shakespeare's timeless tale in a fresh and excitingly relevant fashion. As original cast member Carole D'Andrea would later describe the reaction at the curtain call, "the minute the curtain went up you could feel it . . . they were on their feet with ovations. You could really feel *history,* I swear."

Brooks Atkinson in *The New York Times* remarked, "the author, composer, and ballet designer are creative artists. Pooling imagination and virtuosity, they have written a profoundly moving show that is as ugly as the city jungles and also, pathetic, tender and forgiving." He went on to state that "Everything in *West Side Story* is of a piece. Everything contributes to the total impression of wildness, ecstasy and anguish. The astringent score has moments of tranquility and rapture, and occasionally a touch of sardonic humor."

According to Walter Kerr in the *New York Herald Tribune*, "The radioactive fallout from *West Side Story* must still be descending on Broadway this morning. Director, choreographer, and idea-man Jerome Robbins has put together, and then blasted apart, the most savage, restless, electrifying dance patterns we've been exposed to in a dozen seasons." As far as he was concerned, the choreography pretty much overwhelmed everything else about the show. "Mr. Bernstein," he declared, "has permitted himself a few moments of graceful, lingering melody: in a yearning 'Maria,' in the hushed falling line of 'Tonight,' in the wistful declaration of 'I Have a Love.' But for the most part he has served the needs of the onstage threshing machine."

More unqualified in his praise was John Chapman of the *New York Daily News*, writing, "This is a bold new kind of musical theatre—a juke-box Manhattan opera. It is, to me, extraordinarily exciting . . . the manner of telling the story is a provocative and artful blend of music, dance and plot—and the music and the dancing are superb."

Whatever reservations reviewers might have had were simply hesitancy about just how to treat something that seemed so different than what they expected from the traditional musical theater. The production was a triumph, and by the year's end ticket sales were impressive enough for prices to jump from $7.50 to $8.05. As it was clear that something important had been accomplished in theater, there were reams of newsprint about the show during its run, by both those who wanted to find a tremendous degree of validity in how it brought attention to juvenile delinquency and those who criticized it for trivializing the matter. Some audiences, used to "civilized" evenings of lighthearted entertainment, turned their noses up at what they considered a vulgarization of the "musical comedy" format. Others felt that *West Side Story* had proved that there were no bounds to what topics the genre could approach, when done with this degree of inventiveness and taste. Playwright George S. Kaufman weighed in with an article in the *Times* in which he complained of the creeping trend of seriousness in the musical genre but was quick to add that he thought this particular show was "excellent" in every way.

Despite the show's efforts to address the bigotry the Puerto Rican community faced, one complaint came directly from that group, specifically the lyric in the song "America" describing Puerto Rico as the "island of tropic diseases." As

Dr. Howard A. Rusk pointed out in an article for *The New York Times*, which ran only days after the Broadway opening, the island did not suffer from a large number of diseases, and certainly none that could be attributed to the tropical climate. The lyric stayed for the time being, but would be among those eliminated for the movie adaptation.

The original cast album was produced by Goddard Lieberson and recorded for Columbia Records on the Sunday following the Broadway opening, with the intention of making it available first in Washington and then in Philadelphia prior to its release in New York, starting the first week of October. Adorning the cover were stars Carol Lawrence and Larry Kert exuberantly racing down West Fifty-sixth Street in an image captured by photographer Leo Friedman. The record, which sold for a top price of $4.98, would enter the *Billboard* charts in March 1958 and reach number 5 during the 13 weeks it stayed there. Curiously, despite a lineup of songs that have with the passing decades become standards, there was not a great rush among vocalists to record the tunes.

As a way of publicizing the show and to placate those who might have felt that it was irresponsible to make gang members the focus of a stage musical, Jerome Robbins appeared on the local New York religious series, *Look Up and Live* (WCBS, February 23, 1958). Along with cast members

Carol Lawrence, Larry Kert, and Mickey Calin, Robbins took part in what was billed as a look at "Contemporary Theater and Religion" to discuss the themes and sociological value of the musical with host Reverend Sidney Lanier. As Robbins explained, "love and positive and creative feelings cannot exist in a world surrounded by hostility and violence," without ever trying to put any religious slant on the whole thing. This episode gave television viewers an opportunity to hear four songs from the show, "Tonight," "Something's Coming," "Cool," and a somewhat censored version of "The Jet Song," as performed by the people who had introduced them.

The libretto for *West Side Story* was published by Random House in April 1958, priced at $2.95, an indication that the show had made enough of a mark for its script to be considered saleable in bookstores. Come award season, Carol Lawrence (despite her previous credits) was chosen one of *Theatre World*'s promising newcomers for the year. The New York Drama Critics Circle came up with a tie at first, *West Side Story* and *The Music Man* each receiving nine votes, until a second round of balloting put the latter on top. At the Tony Award nominations announced on March 16, *West Side Story* was selected in the Best Musical category (where Bernstein, Robbins, Laurents, and Sondheim were all included, along with the producers), and for Robbins' choreography, Oliver Smith's scenic design, Irene Sharaff's costumes, and

Max Goberman's work as conductor and musical director; the only acting nominee, Carol Lawrence, was curiously listed in the supporting or featured category despite being the star, as the rules insisted only those billed *over* the title could compete as a lead. At the April 13, 1958, ceremonies Robbins and Smith were the sole winners; the committee selected *The Music Man* for the highest honor.

Plans were already under way to bring the show to London in the fall of 1958, with Robbins once again overseeing the production and British Equity allowing him to use an all-American cast, as this was deemed essential for the flavor and feel of the show. (The last time this had been allowed was for Rodgers and Hammerstein's *Oklahoma!*.) Among the original cast members who would be making the trip overseas were Ken Le Roy (to reprise Bernardo) and both Chita Rivera and Tony Mordente (A-rab), who had wed during the New York run of the show; Rivera left the company when she became pregnant with their daughter (future performer and choreographer Lisa Mordente). Maria would be played by Marlys Watters, Tony by Don McKay (who had filled in for Kert on Broadway while he took a vacation), and Riff by George Chakiris. The terrific advance word from the United States had the West End abuzz with anticipation when the show finally arrived there on December 12, 1958, at Her Majesty's Theatre. The London critics reacted with the same degree of excitement that had greeted the show in New York and *West Side Story* played to capacity houses, becoming one of the great triumphs of the theater season. It was voted Best Foreign Musical by the London Drama Critics, who also cited Robbins and Rivera in their honors. It was clearly the show to see: audiences at the February 25, 1959, performance were startled to find the Queen herself (accompanied by Princess Margaret) in attendance, an event unheralded in advance. The show would have an even longer run in Britain than back home, chalking up 1,039 performances.

After more than a year in New York, *West Side Story* was making way for *Juno*, the upcoming musicalization of Sean O'Casey's *Juno and the Paycock*, which was scheduled to take up residence at the Winter Garden in late February 1959. After moving a few blocks uptown to the Broadway Theater, *West Side Story* had a chance to reoccupy its former digs when *Juno* ended up closing early, due to poor box office. *West Side Story* therefore returned to the Winter Garden on May 11, with plans to close on June 27, 1959, in anticipation of the national tour. (At closing the show had run 732 performances.) Larry Kert was the one principal from the original cast to participate in the tour, which opened at the Philharmonic Auditorium in Los Angeles on July 14. He was joined by Sonya Wilde (and later Leila Martin) as Maria, Thomas Hasson as Riff, Devra Korwin as Anita, and

Carmine Terra as Bernardo. Of note in the company were Eliot Feld (Baby John), Tucker Smith (Big Deal), and Gus Trikonis (Action), all of whom would end up in the film version. The tour proved an incredible success, to the degree that it seemed a mite premature to have closed the show in New York, so plans were made for it to return there in the spring of 1960. Although Larry Kert and Leila Martin were announced in the advertisement heralding *West Side Story*'s Broadway return, once again the failure of a concurrent show altered plans. Carol Lawrence had been signed to costar opposite Howard Keel in the new Harold Arlen–Johnny Mercer musical, *Saratoga*, which was booked into the Winter Garden. When it shuttered there prematurely on February 13, 1960, not only the venue was now available for the *West Side Story* return but Lawrence was as well.

The April 27, 1960, reopening night offered a further incentive for ticket buyers when Leonard Bernstein himself conducted the prologue. The "revival" production also included Hasson, once again as Riff; Allyn Ann McLerie as Anita; and George Marcy as Bernardo. The androgynous Anybodys was played by Pat Birch, who later, as Patricia Birch, would choreograph the stage and film versions of the musical smash *Grease*. That the show had built up such a following that it was able to run for yet another 248 performances (for the final weeks it transferred again, over to the Alvin Theatre) showed that *West Side Story* was rising in popularity and spoke to a wide audience. This boded well for the fact that Hollywood had already come calling with plans to put the property onscreen in a big way.

CHAPTER 3

Hollywood Story

Seven Arts

On April 2, 1958, more than six months into the Broadway run of *West Side Story*, *The New York Times* announced that Seven Arts Productions was the leading contender for the film rights for the show. Because this was a major musical, one likely to be coveted by each of the major studios, many must have been taken aback by the obscurity of the company doing the bidding. The two men behind the recently formed operation, Eliot Hyman and Ray Stark, had been involved with the business end of show business for a few years. Hyman had served as cochairman for Moulin Productions (the company that had produced the 1952 Oscar-nominated *Moulin Rouge*) before starting Associate Artists

Productions, Inc., which distributed British product in America and had purchased the pre–1950 Warner Bros. library for television distribution. In 1956 AAP's parent company, R.P.M., Inc., appointed the former vice president of the Famous Artists Corporation talent agency, Ray Stark, vice president of their West Coast division. Among the organization's varied plans was to create and finance independent films. In December 1957, AAP established Seven Arts Productions to purchase properties to develop into motion pictures. The following year it signed a production, financing, and distribution deal with United Artists. Among the earliest announced projects were adaptations of the Broadway dramas *The World of Suzie Wong* and *Two for the Seesaw*.

In July 1958 it was official: Seven Arts Productions had purchased the motion picture rights to *West Side Story* for $350,000, with a further 10 percent of the worldwide gross to go to its creators after the costs of production had been recouped. By the end of the following year, Stark and Hyman had dissolved their partnership, splitting up the properties they had intended to produce in tandem. The idea was for other companies to handle the actual physical production while Seven Arts retained a coproduction credit. This paved the way for Walter Mirisch and his brothers to enter the scene.

The Mirisch Company

The four Mirisch brothers had come to the entertainment business from various directions. Harold started as an office boy for Warner Bros. in New York before going to Memphis to manage the Warner Theatre. Eventually his older brother Irving joined him. Marvin (who, along with Walter, was actually Harold and Irving's stepbrother) worked in the booking department of a second feature or "B" company, the kind that specialized in grinding out product for the lower half of double bills, called Grand National Pictures. Harold worked his way up to general manager of Warner's Wisconsin circuit of theaters before starting a concession business with Irving, the Theaters Candy Company. While Irving stayed with that side of the business, Harold became chief buyer for RKO Theaters. Through his connections he helped stepbrother Walter get a job as assistant to General Manager Steve Broidy at Monogram Pictures, one of Hollywood's lowliest B companies.

Walter was itching to produce and had his first such credit on the 1947 feature *Fall Guy*, starring Clifford Penn (who was actually Leo Penn, the future father of actor Sean Penn). What really got Walter rolling in the business was his decision to develop a new series for the company, since Monogram was always on the lookout for a lucrative franchise (their standbys in this area include the Bowery Boys and

Boston Blackie). Using a series of children's books from the 1930s, he settled upon *Bomba the Jungle Boy*, which starred Johnny Sheffield, best known as Boy in the Tarzan features. Shot in 8 days and costing all of $85,000, the movie made enough of a profit to prove that Walter was an asset to the firm. In 1951 he was put in charge of production for both the Monogram output and the higher-budgeted pictures under their Allied Artists banner. He coaxed Harold into joining the company, where he would supervise the sales of their Allied Artists presentations. In addition to continuing the *Bomba* films, Walter was given producer credit on such other pictures as *The Rose Bowl Story* (featuring Natalie Wood), *Wichita,* and *An Annapolis Story* (directed by Don Siegel).

Allied Artists' big effort to jump from the second tier to the mainstream came in 1956, when they managed to entice two of Hollywood's hottest directors, William Wyler and Billy Wilder, to make their next pictures for the company, both coincidentally starring Gary Cooper. Wyler's antiwar glimpse into the Quaker lifestyle, *Friendly Persuasion*, would bring respectability to the studio by earning favorable reviews and an Oscar nomination for Best Picture, but the film lost money, as did Wilder's frothy Paris-based comedy *Love in the Afternoon*. While Allied Artists wondered if perhaps they had made a mistake in reaching for bigger bucks, Walter Mirisch was now certain that he wanted to produce "A" list films. Bringing Marvin into the fold, the three Mirisches formed their own independent production firm and managed to land a deal with United Artists to distribute their works.

They started small and safe, with a Joel McCrea western; the actor had already worked in this genre for Walter over at Allied Artists. The premiere effort to carry "The Mirisch Company" credit, *Fort Massacre*, released in 1958, did no more than passable business. Nor was there much profit on their second offering, a more ambitious project in the same genre, *Man of the West* (again starring Gary Cooper, and directed by one of the most revered filmmakers in this field, Anthony Mann). Word, however, had gotten out that the Mirisch brothers were offering creative, hands-off opportunities in hopes of attracting directors fed up with big studio politics. They managed to snag John Ford to helm *The Horse Soldiers*, while Billy Wilder, having had a favorable experience with *Love in the Afternoon* despite its lack of box office success, was happy to offer the company his next project, a Prohibition-era comedy that involved its two leading men cross-dressing for a majority of the picture. Trusting Wilder's instincts and his stellar track record, knowing they had a potentially desirable package with the casting of Marilyn Monroe, Tony Curtis, and Jack Lemmon, the Mirisch Company agreed to finance *Some Like It Hot*, which turned out to be one of the top earners for 1959, finally putting the independent corporation on the map. The following year Wilder delivered a second smash for Mirisch, *The Apartment*, which also brought the organization its first Academy Award winner for Best Picture, solidifying its new position as an industry force to be reckoned with.

In late August 1959, as *Some Like It Hot* continued to produce very lucrative box office results, United Artists handed the *West Side Story* project over to the Mirisch Company, with the understanding that Seven Arts would retain financial interest in the property. (Two other properties would fall under this same arrangement, Robert Wise's eventual follow-up to *West Side Story*, an adaptation of William Gibson's stage hit *Two for the Seesaw*, with Shirley MacLaine and Robert Mitchum; and the Lana Turner melodrama *By Love Possessed*).

Just as Seven Arts had intended, Walter Mirisch decided right off the bat that he wanted Jerome Robbins to be involved in the *West Side Story* stage-to-screen transfer in a major way. But because his only previous Hollywood credit was choreographing *The King and I* movie, it was considered risky to place what was intended to be a pricey production in the hands of someone with no official experience directing a motion picture. The possibility of a codirectorship arose, with the idea that whoever shared the duties with Robbins need not have any considerable expertise in musicals. Instead, someone who had proven himself adept in drama was sufficient, and Robert Wise seemed as good a choice as any. It so happened that Wise was a fan of musicals and jumped at the opportunity to direct one, even if it meant sharing the task. The package was coming together, but slowly; it would be another year before any actual filming began.

Robert Wise

So badly did Robert Wise want to get involved in the motion picture industry in whatever way he could that he had no qualms about trading on nepotism, falling back on his older brother, who had landed a position in the accounting department at RKO Studios. The Indiana native (born in Winchester on September 10, 1914) secured a job as a messenger for RKO's editing department when he was still a teen. There he learned the editing trade, was promoted to the sound editing department, and earned his first professional credit, as the apprentice sound editor on the Leslie Howard–Bette Davis drama *Of Human Bondage* in 1934. He had his first experience with the world of motion picture musicals working on two of the major entries in this genre, *The Gay Divorcee* (1934) and *Top Hat* (1935), both of which starred Fred Astaire and Ginger Rogers. Wise did not, however, actually see his name up onscreen until he worked in collaboration with T. K. Woods on a 1935 short subject, *A Trip Through Fijiland*. He was back behind the scenes of yet another Astaire–Rogers pairing, *Carefree* (1938), as an editing assistant, then finally made the transition to full editor, receiving upfront credit on three major RKO releases, *Bachelor Mother* and *5th Avenue Girl*, both starring Ginger Rogers; and the lavish remake of *The Hunchback of Notre Dame*. Now he was established as one of the studio's chief talents in this field, and the assignments kept coming with the Cary Grant–Irene Dunne hit *My Favorite Husband* (1940); the cult feminist drama *Dance, Girl, Dance* (1940), with Lucille Ball and Maureen O'Hara; and the literate fantasy *All That Money Can Buy* (1941).

Most important was his selection by Orson Welles to be the editor on the fledgling director's first film, *Citizen Kane* (1941), which became one of the landmark motion pictures of all time, its every aspect, artistic, aesthetic, and technical—including the flawless work done by Wise—examined with intense scrutiny and awe by scholars, fans, and future filmmakers. It brought Wise his one Oscar nomination in the editing department. Welles gladly kept him on for his next project, *The Magnificent Ambersons* (1942), but RKO ordered Wise to recut the picture and even direct select insert scenes after Welles had left for South America to work on his (ultimately unfinished) documentary *It's All True*. Unfairly, future film scholars who saw Welles as the ultimate genius mishandled and misunderstood by the crass Hollywood regime would often condemn Wise himself, as if he had crept into the studio overnight and dismantled *Ambersons* of his own accord. Although his contributions to the movie were dismissed, the experience made him realize that there was a great deal more satisfaction to be had in directing and decide to point his career in that direction.

Wise got his chance by accident, when he was assigned to edit one of producer Val Lewton's pictures, *The Curse of the Cat People* (1944). When Lewton became dissatisfied with the work his original designated director, Gunter V. Fritsch, was doing, he fired him and asked if Wise would be willing to take the reins. Confined to a small budget, Wise pulled off a hypnotic fantasy that belied its horror movie title and quickly proved his talents behind the camera. The film would gain something of a cult following in later years. For his reward, Lewton gave him a follow-up, the World War II allegory *Mademoiselle Fifi*, which marked the first time Wise's name appeared onscreen as the sole director. Best of all was his third Lewton assignment, *The Body Snatcher*, a stylish and intelligent thriller starring Boris Karloff. RKO was pleased enough to keep Wise busy, although he stayed in the low-budget realm for the time being, on the relentlessly unsentimental noir *Born to Kill*, another title that grew in reputation over the years. An A western, *Blood on the Moon*, was followed by the film that really established him, the taut boxing drama *The Set-Up*, which was acclaimed for its raw, no-nonsense ambience and streamlined storytelling. Wise earned a critics prize at the Cannes Film Festival and ended up with a contract at Twentieth Century-Fox, a studio with a higher standing within the industry than RKO, which was heading into its decade of decline.

As a director interested in storytelling above everything else, Wise had no desire to be pigeonholed and worked in a variety of genres, including the thriller *House on Telegraph Hill* (1951); one of the most highly regarded of all sci-fi entries, *The Day the Earth Stood Still* (1951); the war film *Desert Rats* (1953), a personal favorite of his; and a comedy, *Something for the Birds* (1952). Independently he set up his own company, Aspen Pictures, in conjunction with Mark Robson and Theron Worth, to direct a documentary-style crime drama, *The Captive City*, distributed by United Artists, and to produce the Gary Cooper vehicle *Return to Paradise* (1953). An assignment over at Warner Bros., a remake of Edna Ferber's epic *So Big* (1953), included among its supporting cast fifteen-year-old future *West Side Story* star Richard Beymer as a student who develops a crush on Jane Wyman. For MGM Wise delivered the all-star ensemble drama *Executive Suite* (1954), the first time he worked with screenwriter Ernest Lehman. Two solid dramas further enhanced his reputation as one of the top directors in the industry, *Somebody Up There Likes Me* (1956; also written by Lehman), considered one of the best of all sports biopics, depicting the troubled life of boxer Rocky Graziano, played by Paul Newman in his breakthrough role, and *I Want to Live!* (1958), an indictment against capital punishment that documented the true story of call girl Barbara Graham's unjustified sentencing to the gas chamber. Susan Hayward won her Academy Award for the film, while Wise earned his first nomination in the directorial category. Between these films was a minor comedy starring Jean Simmons and Paul Douglas, *This Could Be the Night* (1957), which was only significant in that it was the first Wise directorial credit to date that could in any way be described as a musical. Taking place at a seedy New York nightclub, the story was occasionally interrupted for some onstage performances, mostly by cabaret singer Julie Wilson.

At the time Wise was hired by the Mirisch Company and UA to direct *West Side Story* he had just completed the New York-filmed *Odds Against Tomorrow*, which made a statement against racism within the context of a crime caper. It was hardly one of his better efforts, despite its ambitious intentions. Since Arthur Laurents had had nothing but bad experiences working in Hollywood and would unlikely have been any happier on this occasion, it was just as well that Wise chose someone else to do the *West Side Story* adaptation, in the fall of 1959 selecting Ernest Lehman, one of the hottest writers in the business at the time.

Ernest Lehman

Having made his professional writing debut with a profile of bandleader Ted Lewis that he sold to *Collier's* magazine, Ernest Lehman soon became a copywriter for press agent Irving Hoffman. This job consisted of scouring Manhattan for gossip for Walter Winchell and other columnists, which would provide Lehman with plenty of material for one of his seminal film credits, *Sweet Smell of Success*. The characters of scheming press agent Sidney Falco and insidious columnist J. J. Hunsecker first appeared in a short story published in the April 17, 1948, issue of *Collier's*, "Hunsecker Fights the World." By then Lehman had made his first "contact" with motion pictures, having penned a screen story with Geza Herczeg entitled "Silver Creek, N.Y.," which they sold to Republic Pictures. The adaptation, *The Inside Story*, was released in 1948, Lehman's first onscreen mention. (The story was produced yet again, for television, on *Lux Video Theatre* in 1955.) That same year one of his many magazine stories, an exposé of a show business megalomaniac, "The Life of Sammy Hogarth," appeared in the June *Liberty*.

What really brought Lehman attention was his expansion of the "Hunsecker" story, now retitled "Tell Me About It Tomorrow," which ran in the April 1950 issue of *Cosmopolitan*, and his lengthening of the "Hogarth" piece, now called "The Comedian," which appeared in *Cosmopolitan* in January 1952. These led to an offer from MGM and producer John Houseman to adapt Cameron Hawley's novel *Executive Suite* for the screen. Director Robert Wise was pleased with this finished result, which brought Lehman an award nomination from the Writers Guild. Next Billy Wilder asked him to collaborate on the screen version of Samuel Taylor's Broadway hit *Sabrina Fair* (shortened to *Sabrina*). Both movies were among the top box office earners of 1954, and Lehman signed a seven-year contract with Metro that gave him the opportunity to both write *and* direct. He, Taylor, and Wilder earned Oscar nominations and won the Writers Guild Award for *Sabrina*.

Plans for an independent theatrical feature based on "The Comedian" came to naught; the property instead was adapted for television by Rod Serling for one of the most famous of all *Playhouse 90* presentations, with Mickey Rooney in the lead. Similarly, Lehman announced that he was going to write a version of "Tell Me About It Tomorrow" under the title *The Garden of Evil*, but that project stalled until Burt Lancaster and his producing partners enticed Lehman not only to turn it into a screenplay for the Hecht–Hill–Lancaster company but also to consider the possibility of directing it himself. In the meantime Lehman was engaged to bring one of Broadway's most acclaimed musicals, *The King and I*, to the big screen, and it became one of Twentieth Century-Fox's major productions of 1956. Despite losing several key songs along the way, the script was basically faithful to and respectful of what had worked so beautifully onstage, and Lehman was hailed for his adaptation. It brought him a second award from the Writers Guild.

Turning Rocky Graziano's autobiography, *Somebody Up There Likes Me*, into one of the better biopics of the time was another achievement for Lehman and his second collaboration with Robert Wise. When at last came the time for "Tell Me About It Tomorrow" to be filmed, Lehman nearly suffered a nervous breakdown in his efforts to adapt the story to Lancaster's satisfaction and ended up leaving the project before the script was finished. Clifford Odets was brought in to whip it into shape. The idea of Lehman directing was obviously no longer valid, so Alexander Mackendrick did the job. Now called *Sweet Smell of Success* (the intended title of "Tell Me . . ." until the *Cosmo* editors balked at the word "smell"), with Lancaster and Tony Curtis giving among their finest performances, the 1957 release was one of the literate high points of the era. Stark and unsentimental, it contained some of the toughest and most quotable dialogue yet heard onscreen, although Odets received most of the credit for that. It was not, however, the sort of thing most moviegoers wanted to see at the time, so it was up to history to continually raise its stature, and Lehman's reputation along with it. This was enhanced even more so by the sharp and breezy, half-tongue-in-cheek adventure he scripted for Alfred Hitchcock, *North by Northwest* (1959). So perfectly did all the elements fit together that this became the gold standard of all "innocent man on the run" adventures, with many imitators but few peers. It brought Lehman another Oscar nomination for what would be his only original screenplay not based on previously published material. The fact that it was one of the biggest moneymakers of its year was another coup.

So certain was Hollywood that Lehman could adapt pretty much anything and make it work that Fox hired him to turn the nearly 900 pages of John O'Hara's best-seller *From the Terrace* into a relatively comprehensive two-and-a-half-hour melodrama, which proved more commercially that artistically successful. By the time of its filming Lehman was already fast at work on the *West Side Story* script.

To get a fresh perspective on the show, Wise and Lehman caught up with the *West Side Story* touring company while it was in Chicago. Lehman immediately decided there were some aspects of how the play unfolded that did not seem likely to work onscreen. Certain songs would have to be shuffled and repositioned and some of the dialogue trimmed, altered, or censored; additional scenes were to be inserted, but for the most part there was no intention to excise huge chunks of material, as Wise and the Mirisches wanted to stay as faithful in content as they possibly could. Miraculously, not a single song ended up being omitted, a trend quite common and often callously practiced by Hollywood for decades. Many Broadway shows purchased for the big screen had the bulk of the scores that had made them famous whittled down to a number or two, or excised altogether. Indeed, Leonard Bernstein's one previous musical that had been adapted for film, *On the Town*, had kept a mere two songs, plus two dance pieces. The only example prior to *West Side Story* of a movie adaptation keeping every song that had been heard onstage was the 1958 production of *South Pacific*, over which its songwriters, Richard Rodgers and Oscar Hammerstein II, had some control.

The most significant *West Side Story* change from stage to screen was the swapping of the two songs "Cool" and "Gee, Officer Krupke." In the show, in Act I, prior to the "war council" at Doc's store, the Jets had been confronted by Officer Krupke about their "delinquent" ways, prompting Riff to warn his gang to remain "Cool" in light of the harassment by their elders. This was all very well, but Arthur Laurents' insistence on having the Jets sing the blatantly comical

"Krupke" song *after* Riff and Bernardo have just been killed during "The Rumble" had many audience members wondering if perhaps the tone of the number was too frivolous in light of the tragic circumstances. Although Laurents stood by his decision, likening it to the tradition of Shakespeare often following scenes of great tragedy with humorous ones that would alleviate the tension, many, including one of his collaborators, Stephen Sondheim, were certain that the songs should have unfolded in reverse order. The enormous feeling of doom and uncertainty after the two stabbings was far more in rhythm with the explosive nature of "Cool" then the knockabout spirit of "Krupke," and the film would now present them in such a way that future audiences seeing the work done as it was originally intended onstage would often have trouble adjusting.

Maria's joyous abandon over her newfound love for Tony, expressed in "I Feel Pretty," had also followed "The Rumble" onstage, coming as the opening of Act II. Feeling again that this didn't play well when the audience would be wrapped up in the outcome of the violence, Laurents moved it earlier, to the scene in the dress shop prior to Tony's first visit there. That scene would be bracketed by this song and "One Hand, One Heart."

Whereas the Broadway production had followed Tony's rendition of "Maria" with his visit to Maria's fire escape and their duet, "Tonight," Lehman figured there was no harm in placing the song "America" in between to offer a change of scene between the two Tony numbers. "America," however, would not be presented in the same way it had been on Broadway, with Anita and her two friends arguing about the pros and cons of life in their new country. Instead, the brilliant decision was made to turn it into a "battle" between the optimistic women and their more skeptical male partners, who, as Puerto Rican men at the end of the Eisenhower era, had to face rejection and prejudice more frequently in white urban society than their female companions. Stephen Sondheim was enlisted to lyrically revise this particular song more thoroughly than any of the others in the score. The new take on it, and the inclusion of a "dance-off" that now featured the Sharks just as prominently as their women, was truly a masterstroke. The film now had a potent and scathing comment on the truth behind the condescension faced by immigrants in the so-called land of equal opportunity. Even those who would decry the tweaking and rewrites that had been done had to concede that this was an improvement that enhanced the sequence specifically and the musical itself in every possible way.

With his updates, Sondheim was now able to get rid of the controversial knock, "island of tropic diseases," that had caused some outcry from the Puerto Rican community, not to mention the dismissal of Puerto Rico as an "ugly island." The country was now "my heart's devotion" while lines complaining about "the babies crying, and the bullets flying" were gone, replaced by references to "the sunlight streaming and the natives steaming." From that point on, nearly the entire song was different, with an especially sharp back-and-forth of the girls insisting "Life can be bright in America" retorted to by the men's "If you can fight in America," a direct reference to the situation faced in their gang wars, while the line "Life is all right in America" was dismissed by Bernardo and his friends reminding their women, "If you're all white in America." In its own way, this revamping of "America" provided the movie's most memorable and honest rant against bigotry; indeed, it made *West Side Story* one of Hollywood's important statements on the subject up to that time.

Despite a certain degree of permissiveness creeping slowly into American films by the early 1960s, select lines and words that had been heard onstage simply had to be "cleaned up" to appease the censors. Lieutenant Schrank's use of "crap" in the opening confrontation with the warring gangs was now replaced by the less plausible "crud," and a part of Tony and Riff's loyalty oath, "sperm to worm," featured one word that nobody even considered trying to get onscreen in that day and age, so it was revised as "birth to earth." An insult to one of the Sharks' girls about her coming to America "with your legs open" became "with your mouth open," and another taunt by Schrank, asking Action, "How's the action on your mother's side of the mattress?" was deemed a bit too suggestive and turned into "your mother's side of the street." There was apparently an objection to the use of the word "hot" when applied to sex, so during the "Quintet," Anita's anticipatory lyric, "He'll walk in hot and tired—so what? Don't matter if he's tired, as long as he's hot," was changed to "He'll walk in hot and tired, *poor dear*. Don't matter if he's tired, as long as he's *here*." A single line in "The Jet Song," "when the spit hits the fan," was dumped for the safer "let them do what they can."

Further lyric changes were required, not for naughtiness, but simply because of some revisions in staging. Because "I Feel Pretty" was moved earlier in the time frame of the story, the whole scene was taking place not deep in the night, as on Broadway, but at the start of evening. Therefore, "I feel pretty and witty and bright," made to rhyme with "any girl who isn't me tonight," was altered to "pretty and witty and *gay*" requiring the rhyme of "any girl who isn't me *today*." The decision to *not* have Riff and Tony interact during "Quintet" meant that Riff's line, "I'm counting on you to be there, tonight," was gone, so he was heard encouraging Ice with such lines as "We'll be in back of you, boy."

"Ice," in fact, was one of the new names for the film, the equivalent character onstage having been called Diesel. The rest of the Jets retained their stage names, though several of them were never actually called by any particular name during the story, as was certainly the case with a majority of the Sharks. Just for the record, however, the names of Anxious, Nibbles, and Moose used onstage were replaced by Loco, Rocco, and Del Campo. While the idea of keeping any parents from view was held over from the stage presentation, the proprietor of the dress shop in which Maria and Anita toil, Madam Lucia, now made a fleeting appearance onscreen, rather than being merely mentioned in the dialogue.

Although dance would play an important part in the film, it was decided that the highly stylized moment onstage during the song "Somewhere" needed to be rethought. Whereas on Broadway, the walls of the set separated to give Tony and Maria the "open air" they craved in the lyrics, followed by a ballet interlude, they would now simply sing it in the confines of Maria's bedroom. The curious choice on Broadway to have an offstage voice sing the number was, obviously, dispensed with as well.

Perhaps feeling that some dialogue was necessary to verify that the drama was indeed unfolding where the title suggested it was happening, Riff no longer told his fellow Jets that they needed to ask Tony to rejoin the gang because "Against the Sharks we need every man we got," but instead built him up with the line, "He's got a rep that's bigger than the whole West Side."

Satisfied with the script, Jerome Robbins agreed on the idea of sharing the directorial duties with the far more experienced Robert Wise, with the understanding that it would be a mutually agreed-upon give-and-take, with both men okaying the chosen camera angles, setups, shots, and so forth. As far as the Mirisches were concerned, Wise was there to do the dramatic material that did *not* involve anything musical, while Robbins was to make sure the dances worked onscreen as effectively as they had in the theater.

Once it was decided to take the bold risk of actually staging the show's "Prologue" not on a soundstage or a back lot but right on the pavements of Manhattan, Wise and Robbins came together in February 1960 to scout New York locations. Needing something that had a shabby look yet would not be populated by local residents who might interrupt the shooting, they decided that several blocks from Sixty-first to Sixty-eighth Street, west of Broadway, where housing had been vacated in anticipation of the building of Lincoln Center, would fit the bill. Production designer Boris Leven and his set decorator, Victor Gangelin, simply placed curtains in some of the windows and created mock-up shops and storefronts at select points to give it the feeling of a lived-in neighborhood. A playground, however, was essential for the sequence, so one concession was made to allow shooting outside of the titular area, the perfect spot being located at 110th Street between Second and Third avenues. After the "Prologue" and "The Jet Song" were shot in these places, everything else would be filmed on Leven's combination realistic/stylized sets, to be built within the seven soundstages at the Samuel Goldwyn Studios in West Hollywood.

This facility, located at 7200 Santa Monica Boulevard, had started life in 1920 as the home of the long-forgotten Hampton Studios until it was taken over by then husband-and-wife stars Mary Pickford and Douglas Fairbanks with the idea of producing their own films there. They were joined by their cofounder in the United Artists distribution firm, Charlie Chaplin. The studio eventually became the home of independent producer Samuel Goldwyn and was renamed for him in the 1950s. By the end of that decade Goldwyn was producing less and less, allowing other independents to use the soundstages. Among those renting space there was the Mirisch Company. Because of the size and scope of *West Side Story*, the film would pretty much dominate that lot from September 1960 to its completion.

Now that locations were settled upon, it was time to put together a cast.

Starring . . .

In keeping with the assumption that Jerome Robbins was the real "name" behind the project, it was thought at first that no stars would be needed to sell *West Side Story* and that therefore the search for the perfect Tony and Maria would not revolve around a saleable star. For a six-month period various tests were done with no luck. Broadway originals Carol Lawrence and Larry Kert were taken into consideration, but it was decided that they already photographed "too old." Other Marias tested included Anna Maria Alberghetti, Pier Angeli, Suzanne Pleshette, and Susan Kohner. There was even talk in the columns of Audrey Hepburn, though this was probably nothing more than talk, as she had already reached the age of thirty-one by the time filming commenced. Similarly, Elvis Presley's name was bandied about, though it seems unlikely that Wise or Robbins would have ever considered so thoroughly throwing the focus of the piece by this casting. Walter Mirisch saw a test Warren Beatty had made in anticipation of launching his film career and thought he might fit the part quite nicely. Beatty instead landed the lead opposite Natalie Wood in Elia Kazan's *Splendor in the Grass* over at Warner Bros. Wood, in fact, had been brought up by head of casting Lynn Stalmaster as a potential Maria, but nobody pursued this possibility for the time being. Instead, all of the other parts were filled first.

RITA MORENO

Homegrown authenticity had never been required to join the "Sharks" side of the company of *West Side Story*, but Rita Moreno did have the advantage of actually having been born in Puerto Rico, specifically in Humacao, as Rosita Dolores Alviero on December 11, 1931. She was also one of the few actresses of Hispanic heritage who had had a pretty steady run of work throughout the 1950s. Another factor that might have put her on the inside track to portray Anita was the fact that like her character, she had moved from Puerto Rico to Manhattan's West Side, specifically Washington Heights, at the age of five. There she took dancing lessons with Paco Cansino, the uncle of Hollywood star Rita Hayworth. This led to her first professional gig on Broadway, at thirteen years old, in a seven-performance play, *Skylift* (the cast included Eli Wallach) in which she was billed as Rita Cosio. In addition to performing in nightclubs, she was hired to dub Hollywood films for the Hispanic market for young performers like Elizabeth Taylor and Margaret O'Brien.

When she was still a teen she made her motion picture debut in an independent feature, playing a delinquent at a girl's reformatory in *So Young, So Bad* (UA, 1950), an exploitation picture for the B market. This brought her a contract at MGM, where she launched her career as Rosita Moreno (from her stepfather's surname), doing bit parts in *The Toast of New Orleans* and *Pagan Love Song* (singing "Tahiti") before she was dropped. She did manage to get cast in what came to be known as the greatest of all Hollywood musicals, *Singin' in the Rain*, but hardly stood out in a tiny role that required no singing or dancing, as "the darling of the flapper set," Zelda Zanders, a pal of arrogant film star Lina Lamont (Jean Hagen).

As far as the Hollywood casting offices were concerned, Rita Moreno, as she was now known, had an indistinct ethnic look that made her eligible for all kinds of roles, Hispanic or otherwise. She appeared in a B western with songs, *Cattle Town*, as a fiery senorita; *The Fabulous Senorita*, as the Senorita's sister; *Fort Vengeance*, a low-grade Western made for Allied Artists during Walter Mirisch's term there in charge of production, where she got to do some dancing; *The Yellow Tomahawk*, as an Indian named "Honey Bear"; and *Untamed*, as Richard Egan's vengeful, half-breed mistress, memorably telling Susan Hayward, after she has amputated her lover's leg, "What's left of him is mine!" She took a plunge off a cliff after being rejected by Egan in *Seven Cities of Gold*; revised Debra Paget's role of the tragic Indian squaw in the TV version of *Broken Arrow*; showed up as an exchange student from India on an episode of *Father Knows Best*; and was the tavern wench Huguette in Paramount's operetta *The Vagabond King*, where her songs "Vive la You" and "Huguette

Waltz" were dubbed by Eve Boswell. The highlight among these mostly negligible or forgettable credits was being asked to join the cast of Fox's highly prestigious adaptation of the Rodgers and Hammerstein stage hit *The King and I*. As the doomed Tuptim, she got to narrate the "Small House of Uncle Thomas" sequence, which put her into close contact with the film's choreographer, Jerome Robbins. Although she was hardly anyone's idea of an authentic Asian, she was acceptable in the role but was overshadowed by the two stars, Yul Brynner and Deborah Kerr, not to mention the fact that for her one song, "We Kiss in a Shadow," she was dubbed yet again, this time by Leona Gordon.

The film she made just before *West Side Story* was, in a way, the lowliest thing she had appeared in to date; yet it is of interest for the parallels between the two properties. Independently made on a shoestring budget, *This Rebel Breed* (1960) was purchased and distributed by Warner Bros. for the drive-in trade. Because it was not made under a watchful studio eye, the film was actually more raw and gritty in its cry against racially stimulated violence than it might have been, coming from the mainstream. Moreno, receiving top billing in a motion picture for the first time, portrayed a Mexican high school girl whose clandestine relationship with a white boy evokes the ire of her brother, whose Hispanic gang is warring with a Caucasian one. The film not only ended up with Moreno's lover killed but even featured a sequence in which she entered an eatery only to be taunted by some of the white men on hand. In future years, once Warner no longer owned the property, the film was recut to include "nudie" footage inserts and retitled *Lola's Mistake*, a reference to Moreno's character that came off sounding as if she was being criticized for pursuing her interracial romance. Not surprisingly, it was not a credit Moreno (nor a young prestardom Dyan Cannon, in her first movie role) preferred to bring up later on.

To ensure that she came off as well as possible at the *West Side Story* tryouts, Moreno contacted a friend who had already been through the auditioning process and who taught her the dance steps in advance. She fit the part physically, had dance experience, certainly could act, and was a recognizable name. Although she spoke with no discernable accent, she would be required to have one for the film, which, of course, she did effortlessly. Although she would admit to being the "senior" member of the cast, twenty-eight at the time shooting commenced, Hollywood couldn't have offered up a better Anita and the part was hers.

GEORGE CHAKIRIS

Of the five cast principals in the film who rated having their names on the poster advertising, George Chakiris was the only one who had been in the stage version, albeit in London and playing Riff, not Bernardo as he would in the film. Of Greek descent, Chakiris was born on September 16, 1933, in Norwood, Ohio. His family uprooted multiple times, moving from Miami to Arizona and finally to Long Beach, California, where George joined the choir at an Episcopal church. Because of this connection he was hired to sing with them onscreen in MGM's 1947 composer biopic *Song of Love*. Meanwhile, he studied at Hollywood's American School of Dance while attending high school.

Officially calling himself George Kerris but more often than not receiving no upfront credit, he danced in the background of one film musical after another throughout the 1950s, among them the Dr. Seuss fantasy *The 5,000 Fingers of Dr. T*, in the unforgettable dungeon sequence; *The Country Girl*, in the "Land Around Us" production number; and *Brigadoon*, principally in the "Gathering of the Clans" parade. The two most widely noticed of these credits were with grayed hair, backing up Marilyn Monroe in her seminal "Diamonds Are a Girl's Best Friend" number from *Gentlemen Prefer Blondes* (future *West Side Story* dubber Marni Nixon ghosted on some of Monroe's more difficult notes); and dancing behind Rosemary Clooney in "Love, You Didn't Do Right by Me" in the 1954 blockbuster hit *White Christmas*.

He made progress of sorts when he actually received billing (as George Kerris) in the MGM musical *Meet Me in Las Vegas*, not participating in any of the numbers, but playing a young newlywed trying to secure a room at a casino. Also of note was a low-budget independent (subsequently released by Twentieth Century-Fox in 1957), *Under Fire*, simply because it was not a musical but a war film. This indicated that somebody felt he had the potential to function onscreen outside of a song-and-dance context. Even though he played a private whose murder at the end of World War II launches the whole plot, Chakiris did not rate billing.

In 1958 he went to three separate *West Side Story* auditions, uncertain whether he might be cast in the New York or London company. Jerome Robbins selected him for the latter, allowing him to play Riff when the show debuted in December 1958. He would stay for a year and a half, during which time the London offices of United Artists asked him to make a film test, doing two scenes from the show, one as Riff, one as Bernardo (borrowing fellow cast member Ken Le Roy's Bernardo jacket for the filming). Although Chakiris was certain that Riff was the better part, he had no objections when he was informed that Jerome Robbins and Robert Wise wanted him instead to play the leader of the Sharks. The role of Riff would go to someone with more film acting experience.

RUSS TAMBLYN

Few actors remembered for musical roles had as little professional training in the field as did Russ Tamblyn. The son of a supporting and bit-part actor named Eddie Tamblyn (his handful of credits include playing a member of Fred Astaire's band in *Flying Down to Rio*), Tamblyn was born in Los Angeles on December 30, 1934. Although he had taken some dancing lessons when he was a child, he did not pursue the art with any real passion. Instead he began acting on radio during World War II, then in a stage role in *The Stone Jungle*, which brought him two movie offers. The first released, RKO's whimsical allegory *The Boy with Green Hair* (1948), had him (unbilled) watching the picture's star, Dean Stockwell, get those titular emerald locks shorn in a barber shop. The other was one of the mightiest spectacles of the time, Cecil B. DeMille's *Samson and Delilah*, as the young King Saul. Billed as Rusty Tamblyn during this period, he hopped from one role to the next, playing Elizabeth Taylor's kid brother in one of the top attractions of 1950, *Father of the Bride* (and its sequel, *Father's Little Dividend*); the cult favorite, *Gun Crazy*, as the youthful version of future hood John Dall; and *The Winning Team*, as the offspring of Doris Day and Ronald Reagan. His performance in the Republic Pictures Korean War ensemble *Retreat, Hell!*, as a soldier out to avenge his brother's death, so impressed the powers at MGM that they signed him to a contract.

He was a soldier yet again in *Take the High Ground*, his first assignment as an official Metro player, after which he did the first musical that brought him lasting attention in this genre, *Seven Brides for Seven Brothers* (1954). As the youngest of the backwoods Pontipee brothers, Tamblyn, who'd been a gymnast at North Hollywood High School, was called on to do some impressive back flips and quick jumps over an axe handle during the famous barn-raising sequence. He would also do some cavorting with Jane Powell in the "Goin' Co'tin" number, leading many to erroneously believe that he was a trained dancer like his onscreen siblings Tommy Rall, Jacques d'Amboise, Matt Mattox, and Marc Platt. As far as his studio was concerned, he'd done himself proud in this department, no matter what his training, so he was called on again to dance in *Hit the Deck* (1955), performing "Hallelujah" with two singers even less terpsichorean than he, Tony Martin and Vic Damone, and doing a few steps with Debbie Reynolds (his voice, however, was dubbed, not by one "ghost" but two, Rex Dennis and Clark Burroughs); and the George Pal fantasy, *tom thumb* (1958), skipping and prancing about as the title character.

In between he was borrowed by Fox for the much-anticipated adaptation of the biggest best-seller up to that

This publicity shot of Natalie Wood and Richard Beymer duplicated the famous image from the Broadway show that adorned the album and playbill covers.

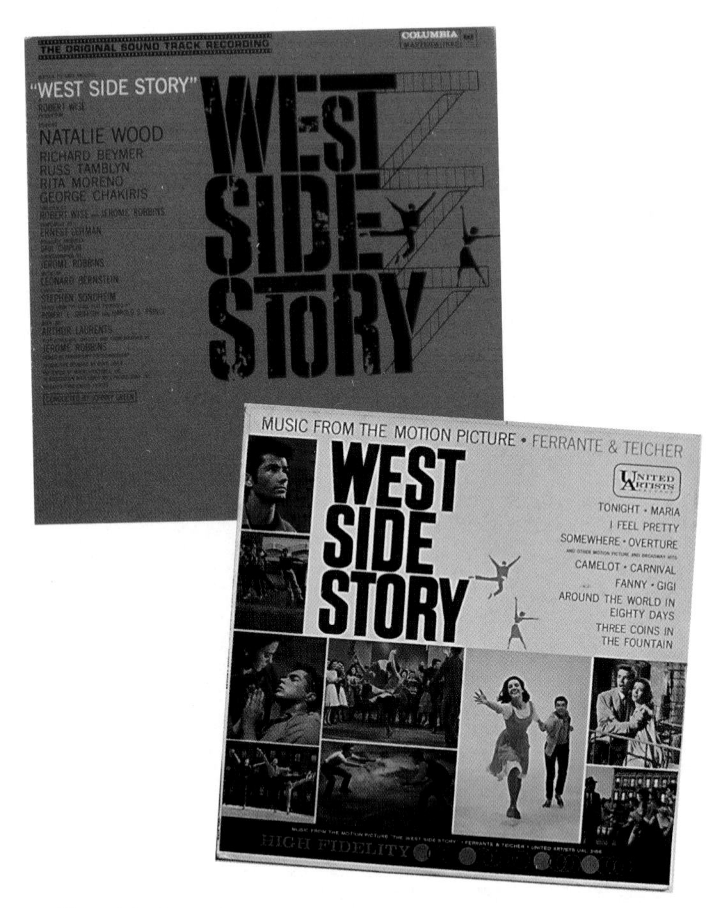

TOP: The original soundtrack album for *West Side Story* on the Columbia Records label spent more weeks at number 1 than any other LP in *Billboard* history.

BOTTOM: Piano duo Arthur Ferrante and Louis Teicher's instrumental album featuring *West Side Story* and other films not only made it into the *Billboard* top 10, but featured the highest charting single released in conjunction with the film, their rendition of "Tonight," which topped off at number 8.

TOP: Jazzman Stan Kenton's renditions of the *West Side Story* score climbed to number 16 on the *Billboard* charts.

BOTTOM: George Chakiris' 1962 album *The Gershwin Songbook*, released on the Horizon label, puts great emphasis on his Academy Award.

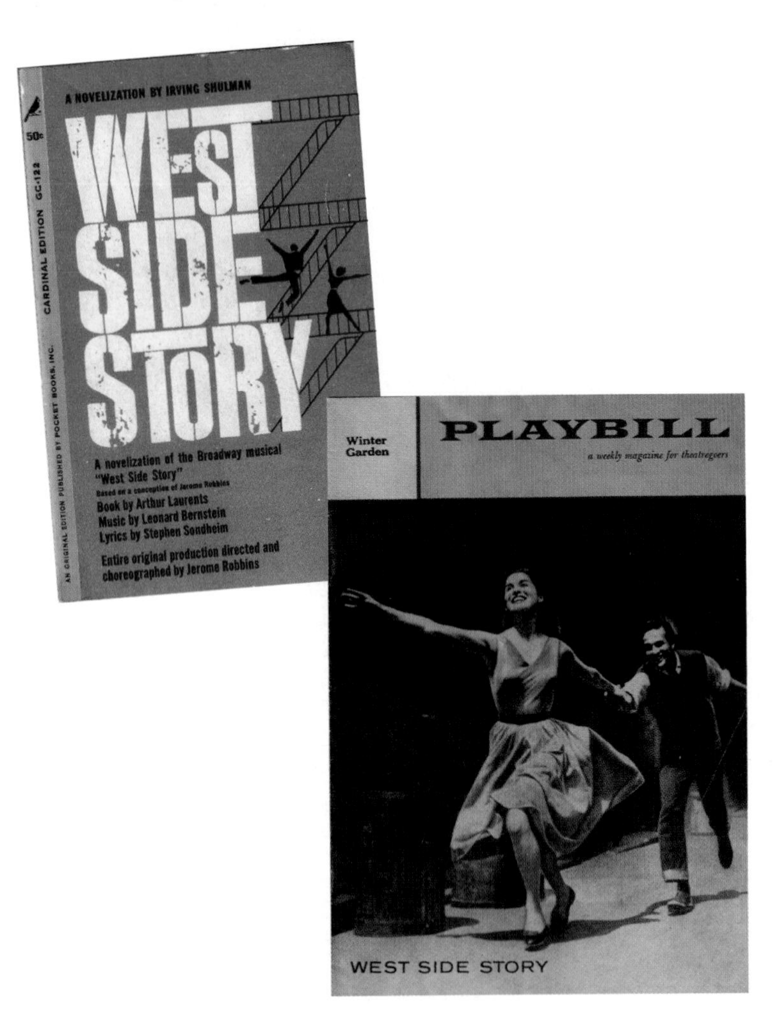

TOP: Irving Shulman's novelization of *West Side Story* took off in a way that most of this ilk never do, staying in print for decades.

BOTTOM: The playbill for the original Winter Garden engagement of *West Side Story*, with Carol Lawrence and Larry Kert.

TOP: The "Dance at the Gym" number includes (squatting on the floor): Russ Tamblyn, Harvey Hohnecker, Tommy Abbott, David Bean, with Gina Trikonis dancing before them. Spotted in the background: Gus Trikonis and John Astin.

BOTTOM: A gathering for a "war council" at Doc's features Eddie Verso, Jaime Rogers (concealed), Richard Beymer, Gus Trikonis, George Chakiris, Ned Glass (concealed), Jose De Vega (concealed), Jay Norman (concealed), Bert Michaels (back to camera, seated), Tony Mordente, Tucker Smith, David Bean, David Winters (concealed), Russ Tamblyn, and Eliot Feld (turned from camera).

TOP: "A Boy Like That/I Have a Love" with Rita Moreno and Natalie Wood.

BOTTOM: On location in New York, Jerome Robbins gives choreographic instruction to three of his Sharks: Jay Norman, George Chakiris, and Eddie Verso.

TOP: "Gee, Officer Krupke" with David Bean, Russ Tamblyn, Tucker Smith, Sue Oakes, Robert Banas, Scooter Teague, David Winters, Bert Michaels, and Tommy Abbott.

BOTTOM: On the playground following the "Prologue" with Tony Mordente, Tucker Smith, Scooter Teague (concealed), Russ Tamblyn, Tommy Abbott (concealed), Simon Oakland, David Winters, and William Bramley.

George Chakiris (back to camera) stabs Russ Tamblyn in "The Rumble" as they are surrounded by (from bottom, clockwise) Bert Michaels (back to camera), Eddie Verso (back to camera), Jay Norman, Jose De Vega, Tucker Smith, David Bean, Tony Mordente, Larry Roquemore, Nick Covacevich, Rudy Del Campo, Jaime Rogers, Eliot Feld, Richard Beymer, David Winters, Harvey Hohnecker, Andre Tayir, Robert Banas, and Gus Trikonis.

time, *Peyton Place* (1957), as the mother-dominated nice guy, Norman Page. The film's tremendous box office returns were further compounded by its nine Oscar nominations, which included a supporting actor nod for Tamblyn. The film exemplified the lush and artificial soap operas Hollywood made a specialty in the late 1950s and early 1960s. More unapologetically sensationalistic was MGM's incredibly silly drive-in melodrama *High School Confidential* (1959), with Tamblyn as a narc masquerading as a student in the kind of archly straight-faced exposé that inevitably became camp with the passing years. After dying tragically as a troubled kid-turned-outlaw in the much-disliked and unnecessary remake of *Cimarron* (1960), Tamblyn was invited to audition for *West Side Story*. Although he was at first under the impression that he was wanted for the role of Tony, he found himself in a more comfortable part, as Riff, gang leader of the Jets. Once again, he would have on-set training in dance, this time by one of the strictest taskmasters, Jerome Robbins.

RICHARD BEYMER

Although the role of Tony would require little more than some finger-snapping and gliding around the gym floor, the actor who ended up with the coveted part, Richard Beymer (pronounced BEE-mer), had actually taken some dance lessons as a child. When he was ten his parents moved from his home state of Iowa (where he was born on February 20, 1938, in Avoca) to a trailer in Los Angeles, where their son landed his first gig on a kids' weekly television show, *Sandy's Dream*. This led to a cattle call audition for producer David O. Selznick, who was looking for a young lad to portray Jennifer Jones' nephew in *Indiscretion of an American Wife*. Getting the role mainly because he had the "same complexion" as Jones, Beymer launched his legitimate acting career in this troubled film that went through various edits and revisions over the years. In the meantime he was seen in the Warner Bros. remake of *So Big* (under the direction of Robert Wise) and then got his "big break" when he was cast as the hero's best friend, Rab, in Walt Disney's *Johnny Tremain*, a whitewashed version of Esther Forbes' novel. Since this was not one of the studio's bigger box office attractions, Beymer went back to being just another actor for hire until director George Stevens decided he had the ideal degree of wholesomeness to portray Millie Perkins' love interest, Peter Van Dam (David Levin had done the role on stage), in Twentieth Century-Fox's prestigious adaptation of the Broadway hit *The Diary of Anne Frank*.

Perkins and Beymer were sincere enough, although their elders acted them both right off the screen, with Shelley Winters taking home an Oscar, Ed Wynn earning a nomination for playing it straight, and one of the holdovers from the stage, Joseph Schildkraut, really making a meal of his part. No matter, the film fared well at the box office, ended up with an Academy Award mention in the Best Picture category, and brought Beymer a contract with the studio, who saw great fan magazine potential. He was, after all, very handsome, very tall, and had just the sort of apple-cheeked look that made him very accessible and unthreatening. After finishing a supporting role in the Bing Crosby comedy *High Time*, as a fellow college student in love with Tuesday Weld, he was summoned to audition for *West Side Story*. With the firm understanding up front that his vocals would be dubbed, he was considered a hot enough new name to placate the producers, who weren't sure if the property alone would justify the money they planned to spend on the movie. That he had bested one of the finalists for the part, Warren Beatty, became something of a thorny issue for the woman who would eventually end up playing Maria, Natalie Wood, but she was nowhere in the picture by the time Jerome Robbins began rehearsing his dancers on May 31, 1960.

THE DANCERS AND THE ADULTS

Faced with the same task he'd had onstage, of finding dancers who could also sing and hopefully act, Jerome Robbins pretty much stuck to those he knew when casting the supporting roles in the film of *West Side Story*. Four dancers who had opened the show on Broadway in September 1957 made the cut: Tony Mordente (now cast as Action instead of A-Rab), David Winters (the original Baby John, now considered too old for that part and therefore taking over Mordente's role of A-Rab), Tommy Abbott (repeating as Gee-Tar), and Carole D'Andrea (in both instances as Jets girl Velma). The show's original Officer Krupke, William Bramley, was also asked to come aboard. Others appearing in the film included David Bean (London's Big Deal, now playing Tiger), Eddie Verso (Baby John in the opening night London cast, now switching sides and playing Shark Juano), Gus Trikonis (like Verso, joining the "enemy," having been a replacement Action on Broadway, now cast as Shark Indio), Gina Trikonis (Gus's real-life sister, promoted from a replacement Minnie to the more prominent character of Graziella), Jay Norman (a replacement Juano, now Pepe), Tucker Smith (who had filled in for Riff, Diesel, and Big Deal in New York, as well as portraying Big Deal in the touring company, now cast as the newly christened character Ice), Eliot Feld (Broadway's replacement and the touring company's Baby John, repeating that role), Harvey Hohnecker (in New York he had stepped in for Gee-Tar; now he became Mouthpiece), Larry Roquemore (like Hohnecker a Gee-Tar replacement, this time becoming a Shark named Rocco), and Jose De Vega (the original Chino understudy and replacement for Juano, now

Chino on film). In a company so filled with motion picture novices, the only other gang member apart from Chakiris with extensive experience dancing for the cameras was Robert Banas (the Jets' Joyboy), who was present in several late fifties musicals including *The King and I*, in the "Small House of Uncle Thomas" sequence under Jerome Robbins' direction; the Columbia cheapie *Calypso Heat Wave*; *Damn Yankees*; and *Li'l Abner*, getting "Stupefied" by Julie Newmar. In a nonmusical vein, he also got mowed down by a reckless driver in an American International Pictures teen flick, *Daddy-O*, the name of which echoed a pivotal bit of slang featured in *West Side Story*.

For the role of Tony's employer, Doc, Polish-born character actor Ned Glass, who was the sort of performer who had been seen off and on in movies for decades, often without billing, proved an ideal choice, providing the right degree of resigned frustration and decency. To play the confrontational Lieutenant Schrank, Robert Wise went with Simon Oakland, an actor he'd previously directed in *I Want to Live!*, where he had played the reporter covering Susan Hayward's trip to the gas chamber. Oakland was outstanding in his few scenes.

NATALIE WOOD

Despite their original intention to fill the cast with unknowns and let the *Story* name sell the picture, it is doubtful that

Robert Wise and Jerome Robbins could have coaxed United Artists or the Mirisch Company into putting together a $5 million-plus film without someone considered a bankable "name." Because Carol Lawrence and others who were *not* of authentic Hispanic heritage had already played the role onstage and the idea of putting makeup on a Caucasian actress and expecting her to do a Spanish accent was not unreasonable or "politically incorrect" at the time, there was basically little worry that Maria be the real deal. When casting director Lynn Stalmaster brought up Wood's name a year before she was finally offered the part, it seemed like a sound and sane choice. She was, after all, currently "hot" within the industry, had basically grown up a part of it, and was well liked among her peers.

Born Natalia Zakharenko (but later simplified to Natasha Gurdin) in San Francisco on July 20, 1938, Wood received her first movie role when she was a mere five years old, dropping an ice cream cone in a fleeting moment in Fox's *Happy Land* (1943). Hollywood found her adorable enough to offer her a real role, playing Orson Welles' daughter in a soapy but popular drama, *Tomorrow Is Forever,* where she was first billed under her newly chosen name of Natalie Wood. She was soon the go-to girl when someone her age was needed to play the offspring of the leading lady or leading man. For the next several years she was the cinematic spawn of such stars as Fred MacMurray (*Father Was a Fullback*), Bette Davis (*The Star*), Bing Crosby (*Just for You*), Margaret Sullavan (*No Sad Songs for Me*), and James Stewart (*The Jackpot*). There was also a more substantial and pivotal role than these, portraying the level-headed little girl who refuses to believe in the existence of Santa Claus in one of the enduring comedies of the 1940s, *Miracle on 34th Street* (1947). Despite the movie's fame and its Oscar nomination for Best Picture, it did not lead to Wood vehicles or turn her into a "child star" attraction.

The film that indicated she was not going to just fade into the sunset like so many kid actors before her was *Rebel Without a Cause* (1955), as the high schooler who turns her back on her family when she feels no love forthcoming from her dad. Thanks to the indelible impression James Dean made in the starring role, as well as the camaraderie between him, Wood, and their "adopted child," Sal Mineo, the movie struck a nerve with teens of the era and became one of the touchstones of "troubled youth" films, as melodramatic as it might seem to modern audiences. Wood, at the age of seventeen, was nominated for an Oscar in the supporting category.

The following year she had another important role in a successful film, *The Searchers*, as the kidnapped frontier girl who ends up adapting to Indian ways until John Wayne shows up to drag her back to her real home. She was thereafter engaged to "carry" her own films, although there was little value to such credits as *The Burning Hills* and *The Girl He Left Behind*, both of which hoped to cause a "fan magazine" stir by placing her opposite Tab Hunter. Warner did, however, hand her the title role in one of their big productions of the late 1950s, *Marjorie Morningstar*, playing a Jewish teen with show business aspirations. Although she strove hard to capture the yearnings of this girl, it is worth noting that Marjorie did *not* make it in show business at the finale. Wood had audience empathy and a certain appeal, even if she was not yet a sure thing as an actress. She struggled with a French accent in the war drama *Kings Go Forth*, where she was upstaged by Frank Sinatra's subtle performance, and then did two more soaps, *Cash McCall*, which she particularly disliked, and the negligible *All the Fine Young Cannibals*, where at least she got to act opposite her then-husband, Robert Wagner.

Everything fell into place nicely with *Splendor in the Grass*, which offered a challenging script by William Inge that actually had the guts to criticize the puritanical and wrong-headed condemnation of premarital sex that was the prevalent attitude in motion pictures at the time. Working under one of the most admired directors in the industry, Elia Kazan, Wood rose to the occasion, going from gleefully happy to suffering a nervous breakdown, ending up embittered and disillusioned over how parental interference and archaic beliefs have laid waste to her seemingly idyllic romance with the high school football star. With Wood's marriage to Wagner breaking up, her onscreen affair with co-star Warren Beatty eventually became the real thing. Wood was certain that Beatty stood an excellent chance of securing the starring role in UA's upcoming film of *West Side Story*.

Instead, it was Wood who was asked to participate in late July 1960, only days after she had turned twenty-two and two weeks before the picture would finally commence filming in Manhattan. (Coincidentally, fan magazines had reported back in 1958 that Wood and Wagner had attended *West Side Story* during their honeymoon in Manhattan.) Although Wood was not required to be in any of the scenes shot back east, she had a small window of time in which to prepare for a part she was a tad hesitant about accepting. She would, after all, be required to speak with a convincing Spanish accent, do some dance steps, and sing a very challenging score by Leonard Bernstein and Stephen Sondheim. It was, however, a great role in what was being talked up as one of the major productions of the new decade, and she accepted an upfront salary of $250,000 to do it, with the assumption that she would work hard with a vocal coach to conquer the songs and sing them herself. Robert Wise, Jerome Robbins, the Mirisch Brothers, and United Artists were willing to placate her with the understanding that if the vocal tracks she recorded were not up to par she might be "helped" by a ghost singer. The film's chosen musical supervisor, Saul Chaplin, however, knew she was never going to hit all the notes required and had decided from the get-go that he would engage someone else to sing all of her tracks.

NEW YORK CITY

Robert Wise and Jerome Robbins journeyed east with their Sharks and Jets, plus Krupke and Lieutenant Schrank, to put the two opening numbers, "Prologue" and "The Jet Song," on film using authentic New York City backdrops. According to Walter Mirisch, it was Robbins who, early in the project's inception, had to be talked into the location filming, thinking that his work was simply too stylized to play believably against real buildings and city blacktops. Wise, however, was adamant that this was how the movie should be presented. (A trial run in downtown Los Angeles, in which the Jets went into their moves as a playback of the Bernstein score emanated from the back of a truck, drew nothing but dumbfounded and hostile reactions from onlookers, which might have been another reason to doubt this stylized approach would work in a realistic setting.)

Actual shooting commenced on West Sixty-eighth Street on Wednesday, August 10, 1960, filming George

Chakiris and fellow Sharks Jay Norman and Eddie Verso forming their trio in advance of spinning up the street and then striking their famous raised-leg pose (which became among the most memorable and reprinted images from the movie). This was followed by the enemy gangs leap-frogging over one another in an alley. It was evident from the word go that the perfection Robbins strove for in the theater, often crossing the line from discipline to sadism in the opinion of many who toiled under his lash, was going to be his goal on film as well. Robbins let it be known that he wanted nothing less than the best for each take and was insistent on trying every camera angle and possible dance move repeatedly. Worried that preserving his vision on film meant there was no going back and fixing it later, Robbins put the movie behind schedule faster than anyone expected. The weather was often uncomfortably hot and the cast was under pressure to deliver 100 percent, take after take. Wise and Robbins maintained a professional relationship, although the former, who was officially serving as producer as well, made it clear that directorial indulgence at the expense of getting the picture done was not his manner of working. Wise had more experience in the technical side of what could and could not be accomplished, while Robbins saw no reason not to repeat attempts if it meant achieving something extraordinary.

The image of sneakered gangs pirouetting about the Manhattan streets was undeniably fresh and striking, but it was not easy on those doing the steps. "Of course it's always more difficult to dance on a hard surface," Chakiris would later observe. "Ideally you want a floor that gives a little, otherwise your legs are getting that much more pressure and punishment."

The location shoot was supposed to conclude on August 24 but ended up stretching out to five weeks. (One scene involving Anybodys begging Riff to let her join the Jets actually required reshoots in Hollywood, with a backdrop recreated to match the authentic New York site, months down the line). During that time Wise, his cameraman, Daniel L. Fapp, and assistant director Robert E. Relyea discussed how they might plunge audiences into the piece in a way that would not depend upon the traditional pan down from the urban skyline that was the norm in films set in Manhattan. They settled upon a direct, bird's-eye view shot from a helicopter, the camera capturing New York City in a way few people had ever even imagined before. With Wise and crew simply pointing the camera downward as they flew over the ever-moving metropolis, such familiar sites as the Empire State Building, the United Nations, Columbia University, and Yankee Stadium appeared with an almost eerie sense of distance and calm. It made for a truly smashing opening and let audiences know immediately that what was about to unfold was out of the ordinary.

HOLLYWOOD

Back in Hollywood, Natalie Wood did her best to keep up with the experienced dancers during rehearsals, although she was not require to participate in anything as strenuous as they had to do. She would swirl about during "I Feel Pretty," do the finger-snapping glide about the gym floor with the equally undertrained Richard Beymer, and repeat similar moves in a solo bit added for the film while awaiting news of the Rumble on her tenement rooftop. Although many in the cast were initially unimpressed by the star in their midst, she soon proved herself a trouper and endeared herself to the company by her lack of pretentiousness. Indeed, she got along famously with Jerome Robbins once he began to work with her, despite her lack of skills in the field at which he excelled. The one person for whom she held absolutely no affection turned out to be Beymer, whom she pretty much cold-shouldered throughout the shoot. Fortunately their love scenes on camera did not suffer as a result, their excitement over each other conveyed convincingly for movie audiences who were none the wiser about the real-life animosity.

Now settled in for the remainder of the shoot at the Goldwyn Studios starting on September 12, Robbins continued his meticulous manner of directing with two of the most challenging and exciting dances, "America" and "Cool." The former consisted, according to Rita Moreno, of choreography for the girls devised by Peter Gennaro, while Robbins concentrated on the boys who had now been added to the number. Despite the listing in the final credits of four dance assistants, Gennaro would not be acknowledged onscreen. "America" turned out to be one of the outstanding revisions from the stage production, a fiery duel involving George Chakiris and Rita Moreno and their backup cohorts that was thrilling as a dance piece but also brought out the best in both actors, as Robbins was choreographing to their characters' personalities. It was perhaps this scene more than any other that contributed to the awards they would win. (Curiously, despite perfectionism, the sequence contains a quick and distracting glimpse of the soundstage ceiling.)

"Cool" was rethought for a claustrophobic indoor car park, with headlights and a low ceiling adding to the tension but also contributing to the discomfort and exhaustion felt by the participants. As was much reported, Eliot Feld (Baby John) ended up succumbing to pneumonia as a result of filming this number. "When we finished 'Cool' we were so happy," David Winters told documentary filmmaker Peter Fitzgerald, "that we took our kneepads . . . and put them in trash cans and burned them."

The Mirisch Brothers and United Artists soon found themselves in a quandary. They had to admit that they were very excited about the footage coming from the shoot, but they were worried that the budget was already being stretched by Robbins' painstaking working habits. "Having two directors, which seemed like a very good idea in concept," Walter Mirisch explained in the 1995 documentary *West Side Stories*, "led to a great deal of time spent in discussion between the two directors . . . we began to feel that perhaps we had too many cooks." Figuring that Robbins' choreography had already been worked out in advance and that the bulk of the difficult dance sequences had already been finished, they made a decision that would give those from the theater community further reason to believe that Hollywood was the devil simply around to chew up and spit out the real artists.

Around October 25, while "Dance in the Gym" was being staged, Jerome Robbins was dismissed from the project. As far as UA was concerned, Robert Wise could carry on without him. Wise, however, was insistent that Robbins have some further say in the end result. Therefore, he generously extended the invitation for his codirector to look at the footage of what he had shot following his departure and make suggestions. If he felt that what he was seeing stayed close enough to his vision, he could decide if he wished to keep his codirectorial credit. Because three of his credited assistants, Tony Mordente (the film's Action), Tommy Abbott (Gee-Tar), and Margaret Banks stayed on, they would be responsible for ensuring that his unmistakable style was upheld in the staging. (The fourth assistant, Howard Jeffrey, departed with Robbins.) Mordente had the great idea to toss some of Russ Tamblyn's tumbling moves into the "Dance in the Gym," which proved to be among the scene's highlights.

Needless to say, the cast was devastated by this turn of events. Robbins might have worked them hard, but they had to admit that what he was doing was succeeding splendidly. Although some might have dismissively thought he was simply around to make the picture work *musically*, the company was quick to point out that he did work with them closely on their performances as well. In contrast, Wise was the kind of director who stood back and let his performers find their way with as little interference as possible. He would get the job done and was never less than gentlemanly to work with, but the cast would now have to soldier on without the far more demanding, and therefore more personal, efforts of Robbins. Almost the only cast member who ended up having very little to no interaction with him was Richard Beymer, who later expressed a certain degree of relief, so unsure was he about being able to deliver the goods. Because of the turn of events, he therefore avoided the close scrutiny of a director who might not have been as willing as Wise to accept his work.

Different sources would speculate on what percentage of the picture had been completed to satisfaction up to this point: 40 percent, 60 percent, or as much as 80 percent. In any event, despite the assumption that production would now zip along, filming of *West Side Story* continued for nearly 4 additional months. (There was even a brief trip outside the studio for a shot in the "Quintet" number of the Jets walking under a highway bridge that was reportedly done in downtown Los Angeles.) When shooting finally concluded in February 1961, an estimated $6.8 million had been spent, a cost increase of close to $2 million. If some members of the company had been made uneasy by the firing of the musical's originator, further tension arose when it became clear that a great deal of vocal dubbing would be done to ensure that viewers did not feel cheated by actors who couldn't meet the demands of the score.

MARNI NIXON AND THE DUBBERS

Certainly one reason the average moviegoer never gave much thought to who was doing the actual singing for "non-singing" actors was the fact that Hollywood made sure to keep it hush-hush and let those who bought the illusion assume that everybody who managed to achieve any level of fame in movies had also been extremely well trained at singing. Of course, the reality was quite different. Not only were plenty of performers dubbed throughout the history of talking cinema, but it became the custom for people singing onscreen to vocalize to a playback track on the set, making sure their lip-synching would match what had already been recorded. Therefore, even the best singers were, by necessity, being dubbed, albeit by themselves. The frequent need of motion pictures to find better singers to pipe in for contract players and established stars, however, often evoked the ire of those who felt that "real talents" were being deprived of the chance to shine onscreen in favor of actors lacking in this particular ability. The trick was finding people whose singing style came close to the actor's speaking voice, therefore making the "deception" more believable and something that need not draw any attention.

For years most movie musicals were cast with performers from the singing profession. There were only rare instances of "serious" actors who actually could carry a tune when called upon, Irene Dunne and Jane Wyman being good examples. As far as Hollywood was concerned, if a role required a box office name or somebody who was dramatically ideal for the part, whether or not that person could sustain a note was of secondary importance. What did it matter if two of the most adept ladies on the dance floor, Rita Hayworth and Cyd Charisse, always required "ghosts" to get them by on the songs? Few outside the industry knew of it or questioned it, much to Hollywood's delight.

Indeed, one of the rare times when the industry itself drew attention to a dubbed voice was MGM's 1954 version of *The Student Prince*. When star Mario Lanza proved difficult and needed to be replaced, the studio had the advantage of having already prerecorded his vocal tracks. His voice, after all, was why people attended Mario Lanza movies, so the solution was simply to find somebody else to move his lips to Lanza's singing. Figuring it was best not to tempt fate by having a box office attraction be seen while Lanza's recognizable voice was heard, MGM cast a newcomer, Edmund Purdom, to play the part. Since nobody was primed to show up for an Edmund Purdom picture, the ads played up the credit "and the singing voice of Mario Lanza."

Deborah Kerr made no apologies for the fact that she couldn't sing, but she certainly did not want that to prevent her from playing a role so otherwise suitable to her talents as Anna Leonowens in *The King and I*. Twentieth Century-Fox wanted her and assured her up front that she could work with a professional singer to ensure that the shifts between herself and her dubber were pretty seamless. Marni Nixon was hired for the task, but it was contractually understood that the credits would never mention her participation, something she'd been used to.

Because she ended up "ghosting" on three of the most famous and widely attended movie musicals of all time, Marni Nixon was one of the rare singers to toil in this "behind-the-scenes" field who became quite well known in her own right. Nixon (born Margaret Nixon McEathron in Altadena, California on February 22, 1930) had originally intended playing violin to be her career, until she realized how much more skilled she was at singing. Along the way, she had already gotten her first taste of the movie industry, doing extra work and even landing a recurring role at RKO in a series of films starring radio comedians Lum and Abner. Becoming a member of the Roger Wagner Chorale brought her back to pictures and to her first experience of singing offscreen when the group (which included Marilyn Horne) was engaged to provide the heavenly chorus heard by Ingrid Bergman in RKO's 1948 epic *Joan of Arc.* Around that same time she secured a job as a messenger on the MGM lot; this brought her into contact with composer Bronislau Kaper, who hired her to dub Margaret O'Brien "singing" a Hindu song in a scene from *The Secret Garden* (without even meeting the actress or seeing the clip of film beforehand). Although she achieved fame within the world of classical performing (including appearances at Tanglewood, which brought her into contact with Leonard Bernstein), it was winning *Arthur Godfrey's Talent Scouts* that gave her her widest public recognition, appearing on his radio and television show several times. In the meantime, Fox hired her to dub some notes that were out of Marilyn Monroe's range in the famous "Diamonds Are a Girl's Best Friend" number from *Gentlemen Prefer Blondes* (a scene featuring George Chakiris) and she showed up in the chorus of Broadway's *The Girl in the Pink Tights*.

Her assignment as Deborah Kerr's vocal ghost on *The King and I* was a major one. Although she was paid very little and had resigned herself to being an unknown once again, this became a rare instance of the cat being let out of the bag, when Kerr herself casually made public mention of Nixon's participation. The very next year Nixon was filling in for the same actress for some songs in *An Affair to Remember*.

Although Natalie Wood was under the impression that she would be doing her own singing in *West Side Story*, Nixon was engaged to be present during the prerecording of Wood's tracks in order to get a sense of how the star would be singing the role, which made the already intimidated actress even more certain that she was not going to fulfill her wishes of doing the part completely on her own.

The directors having placated Wood throughout the shoot meant that Nixon had a difficult task when the time finally came for her to record Maria's vocals. Not only would she have to imitate Wood's Spanish-accented speaking voice, but she was also required to match the actress's lip movements (called "looping" in industry terminology), rather than the onscreen performer trying to match the dubber's prerecorded vocal in the customary way. Nixon was also called on to sing during "Quintet" for Rita Moreno, meaning that the number would feature her "portraying" both Maria and Anita. As previously, Nixon was hired with no assumption that she would receive any credit for the job she did. Nor would her name be seen anywhere on the soundtrack album. In another example of Leonard Bernstein's generosity, Nixon's request to have some percentage of the record sales was finally solved when the composer suggested he relinquish one quarter of a percent of his own royalties to the singer, a move that benefited her tremendously in light of the album's amazing success. (Three years later would come her third famous dubbing assignment, ghosting for Audrey Hepburn in *My Fair Lady.*)

Because of Nixon's participation in "Quintet," Anita would have *three* different singing voices. Although Moreno was engaged to do her own vocalizing on "America," the low register required for "A Boy Like That" was beyond her reach. Betty Wand was hired as a "standby" vocalist but was officially paid as a bit player, as opposed to a singer. Wand had done her share of dubbing in the past, including Esther

Williams in *Easy to Love*; Kay Kendall in *Les Girls*; Rossano Brazzi's *male* offspring in "Dites Moi" in *South Pacific*; and most notably Leslie Caron in *Gigi*. Because Wand wasn't able to benefit from Bernstein's or anyone else's kindness with regard to royalties, she later took her case to court (in February 1963), filing suit against B & P Productions (Robert Wise's production company) and Columbia Records, complaining that she was never given a genuine salary for her task or proper credit and demanding $60,000 in damages. The suit was eventually settled for an undisclosed sum. This might have made Wand happy, but one person who remained forever dissatisfied with the decision to have someone else interpret "A Boy Like That" was Rita Moreno, who hated the manner in which Wand sang the song, claiming she was striving to sound too perfect, when her own more angry rendition would have worked better.

Jimmy (or Jim) Bryant (born in Birmingham, Alabama in 1929) did the vocal dubbing for Richard Beymer, a decision made at the start. Bryant had attended the Birmingham Conservatory for Music before heading to New York, where he worked as a background singer. In 1956 he moved west, landing a job playing bass with the house band at Frank Sinatra's Puccini's restaurant in Beverly Hills. After several auditions the *West Side Story* job was his, although unlike Wand and Nixon, he did not do this kind of thing frequently.

In fact, his only other musical credit of note would come six years later, filling in for James Fox in *Thoroughly Modern Millie*. Bryant's interest in music was more instrumental and he became an orchestrator, working in several instances with John Williams.

More curious was Saul Chaplin's insistence that Russ Tamblyn have his vocals on "The Jet Song" dubbed by one of his costars, Tucker Smith, who was cast as Jets member Ice. This meant that Smith would be visible onscreen in the same scene in which his voice was coming from another cast member's mouth. Tamblyn was no happier about this than Wood and Moreno were, but at least got to use his own voice on "Gee, Officer Krupke," which he did quite splendidly.

Something's Coming

Despite his expulsion from the project, Jerome Robbins most certainly wanted some say in how the finished product was going to look, and accepted Robert Wise's offer to come back and look at the footage that had been shot since he left. Wise had no delusions that he had the sort of expertise in musical staging that Robbins did. Robbins suggested cuts and re-edits of sequences, principally "Dance at the Gym," in order to ensure that the competitive nature of the Sharks and Jets was made clear to audiences. The codirector credit would therefore be retained, with Wise, as the film veteran and the one on the project from start to finish, receiving top billing. Although it is doubtful that a perfectionist of Robbins' level would ever be fully happy, clearly he felt something had been done right to retain credit on the picture. Whatever the dissensions, Wise insisted on being optimistic. "I think it worked out all right," he told *The New York Times* shortly before the movie debuted. "We got the benefit of Robbins' choreography and he got the codirecting credit he wanted. He says he's happy with the final picture. So am I."

In mid-March 1961, while the film was still in the early stages of postproduction, ads began appearing in *The New York Times* trumpeting the reserved-seat engagement at Manhattan's 1,545-seat Rivoli Theatre on Broadway at Forty-ninth Street, to begin on October 18. In the honored tradition of show business hyperbole, the ads stated, "The Mirisch Company proudly announces the world premiere of one of the great entertainments in the history of motion pictures." Advance tickets were offered ranging from a $3.50 top price for the orchestra and loge at the Friday, Saturday, Sunday, and holiday showings to $1.50 for the highest seats in the balcony at the Wednesday matinees. *West Side Story* was scheduled to run at 8:30 each night, with 2:30 matinees on Wednesdays, Saturdays, and Sundays and an additional showing on Saturday at 5:15, which also qualified as a matinee. Special New Year's Eve prices of $6.00, $5.00, and $4.00

were offered. In just the first week of availability, advance ticket sales reached $30,675.85.

This advance sales ad was also among the first glimpses moviegoers would get of the simple yet unforgettable logo Saul Bass had come up with for the picture. Tattering the title lettering to suggest the deglamorized urban setting, Bass then stacked the three words atop one another and joined them on the right side with a fire escape, upon which danced two sticklike figures, presumably Tony and Maria, although the bulk of the dancing would be done by other characters in the film. The actual poster was made that much more striking by the deep red background against which the black letters appeared. Bass, who had just recently created for director Otto Preminger such bold images as the broken body for *Anatomy of a Murder* and the raised rifles against a flaming background for *Exodus*, had once again captured a work perfectly, and the logo would become the defining one for *West Side Story* in general.

Tonight

Because of where it was set and where it originated, *West Side Story* had its glittering premiere in New York City rather than in Hollywood. The October 18, 1961, opening night was a benefit showing for the Henry Street Settlement, with actual public screenings to begin the following day. "Tonight!

Tonight! It all begins tonight!" heralded the ads in that Wednesday's papers. *West Side Story* would be competing for audience attention with such newly released attractions as Spencer Tracy and Frank Sinatra in the drama *The Devil at 4 O'Clock*, which opened that same week, at the Criterion; MGM's Jesus epic *King of Kings*, at the State; one of the seminal comedies of the era, *Breakfast at Tiffany's*, starring Audrey Hepburn, at Radio City Music Hall; the Susan Hayward remake of the hoary melodrama *Back Street*, at the Capitol; Paul Newman in a career peak with the screen's definitive look at pool sharks, *The Hustler*, at the Paramount; Federico Fellini's controversial *La Dolce Vita*, at the Henry Miller; and another picture starring Natalie Wood, *Splendor in the Grass*, which had only just made its long-overdue debut the week prior, at the Victoria. Prerelease interest continued to build in the months leading up to *West Side Story*'s debut and advance sales had hit $165,000 by opening day.

When the curtains parted to accommodate the magnificently large Panavision 70 screen at the Rivoli, first night viewers were treated to something more than just the customary overture. Robert Wise had not wanted audiences shuffling about and talking during the overture and therefore had his visual effects specialist Linwood Dunn design an abstract pattern that looked like something akin to "a 1950's computer program card," as Richard C. Keenan so astutely put it in *The Films of Robert Wise*. This was enhanced by gradual color changes until the camera began to slowly track away to reveal the title of the film as Bernstein's pulsating music created the tone of excitement and danger. Only then did the lights come down to begin the awesome overhead views of New York that Wise and his team had concocted. The next two and a half hours would fly by with a cinematic bravado that confirmed the decision not to include an intermission break was a sound one.

If the film did not garner across-the-board raves (and how many movies do?), it mattered not at all because those who loved it did not hesitate to use the word "masterpiece." This was not just another Broadway musical transferred to the screen for viewing pleasure; it created the instant feeling of something far better having been accomplished.

Bosley Crowther in *The New York Times* stated his enthusiasm right up front. "What they have done with *West Side Story* in knocking it down and moving it from stage to screen is to reconstruct its fine material into nothing short of a cinema masterpiece." He continued, "The drama . . . which cried to be released in the freer and less restricted medium . . . is now given range and natural aspect on the large Panavision color screen, and the music and dances that expand it are magnified as true sense-experiences."

Positive advance word had already come from *Variety* back in September, following press screenings. "*West Side Story* is a beautifully mounted, impressive, emotion-ridden and violent musical which, in its stark approach to a raging social problem and realism of unfoldment, may set a pattern for future musical presentations. Screen takes on a new dimension in this powerful and sometimes fascinating translation of the Broadway musical to the greater scope of motion pictures." The praise for Robbins' contributions could not have been higher: "His dancing numbers probably are the most spectacular devised and lensed, blending into story and carrying on action that is electrifying to spectator and setting a pace which communicates to the viewer." While being most impressed with George Chakiris among the cast, the paper conceded that Natalie Wood gave "an entrancing performance," that Rita Moreno "scores hugely," and, proving that reviewers could also be taken in by the magic of movies, said Richard Beymer "impresses with his singing" (oops).

The *New York Herald Tribune* called it "The film that must not be missed this year. . . . The American genius for movie musicals has been excitingly reasserted with *West Side Story,* which even among the best of the breed is unique, at least five years ahead of its time, and shows its creators' disposition not to follow history but to make it . . . the pure animal energy at times overflows the screen." Of the principals, they proclaimed Natalie Wood "splendid" and Richard Beymer a "nice combination of modesty and rapture," and concluded that Rita Moreno "all but takes over the picture."

According to *Journal American*, "*West Side Story* sets a new high for screen musicals," while the *New York Post* declared, "Never before has the full scope of the new larger screen been so fully utilized." *Life* weighed in by calling it "The most adventurous movie musical ever made"; the *New York Mirror* hailed it as "the peer of movie musicals" and the *New York World-Telegram and Sun* labeled it "a dynamic entertainment with box-office success written all over it."

Far more inconclusive was *Time*, whose critic simply couldn't get over the fact that the movie wanted to show restless youth in a favorable light. "Sociologically, the film bids to be taken seriously," the review stated, "but *West Side Story* goes wildly, insufficiently wrong when it insists that society is entirely guilty, that the teen-age hoodlums are ultimately innocent." Making it quite clear that the reviewer was also underwhelmed by the source material, the article still managed to compliment the adaptation, stating that "Under Robert Wise's driving direction its set pieces are socko and incessant," but, in a major slap in the face to a score that has since become iconic, insisted that "Leonard Bernstein's music, as usual, spinelessly eclectic, fails (as the whole film fails) to merge the moods of sweetness and blight, but it is often swell strutty stuff." Robbins, however, was singled out once again for praise, his choreography described as "possibly the most gorgeously galvanic sequences of dances ever caught on celluloid."

Films in Review weighed in with the most damning of reviews, although it began on a complimentary note: "Technically, *West Side Story* is one of the most interesting motion pictures of the last decade." Then they quickly dismissed the film, claiming that "emotionally, intellectually, and culturally it's so confused it's self-defeating." This was not a condemnation of a motion picture botch of a great stage work but a putdown of the whole enterprise, calling Jerome Robbins' choreography "totally unrelated to a slum, racial tensions, subnormal mentalities, and degraded living habits," deciding it was "false factually, and unintegrated dramatically, *West Side Story* is specious, even as entertainment." Clearly, like *Time*, the magazine was looking for a stark and realistic examination of slum conditions and had no patience for artists finding compassion in the young. *Films in Review* also had its complaints about certain cast members, stating, "Natalie Wood isn't up to it" and pointing to "equally serious miscasting with Richard Beymer." Tamblyn was also shot down as the "wrong choice" because of his cherubic countenance, while Chakiris was commended for "acting with acuity and style" and Moreno was championed for acting "with seemingly personal feelings."

Indeed, the one cast member who came in for the greatest critical trouncing was Beymer, whom many felt wasn't particularly convincing as someone who had formerly run with a gang, let alone led one. Beymer hadn't exactly established himself up to that point as much more than an affably boyish, lightweight fellow with a handsome, shiny face and wavy hair. *West Side Story* would, in truth, represent his best effort in front of the camera, as he certainly played the part with passion and empathy, mouthing to his ghost vocalist with the right degrees of longing and qualified hope. He was sympathetic and in no way did a disservice to the great film in which he was appearing. However, harkening back to Jerome Robbins' "actor friend's" dilemma about Tony's counterpart, Romeo, and how to infuse such a seemingly passive character with sufficient life, Beymer simply hadn't the chops to make something great out of the part and wound up handing over most of the picture to the edgier characters around him. Certainly, Beymer himself had no fondness for his performance, walking out on the Royal Command Performance of the picture when it opened in London in 1962, blaming his discomfort with watching himself. "My character was so weak," he would later complain. "I mean, there I was in Todd A-O walking around on my tip toes." He added, "I had my chance, and it didn't click. The movie did."

Russ Tamblyn had no reason to believe that his handful of detractors were correct in their lack of enthusiasm. Tamblyn had always registered well onscreen and he seized this golden opportunity with tremendous gusto, giving Riff the requisite tough-guy personality and a sense of persuasiveness and command that made him a more convincing leader than Beymer's Tony. Managing to keep up with the trained dancers, bouncing smoothly and excitingly among them, he easily pulled focus with his dazzling flips through the air and his swooping dismount from a bar during "The Jet Song." That there was a feeling of loss when he exited the picture long before the wrap-up was a testament to how much strength he had brought to it.

Not only receiving the expected top billing but also having her name printed in a typeface that much larger than the other principals' names, Natalie Wood fully justified her status as the most recognizable star attraction in the production. Although costar Moreno was quick to trash Wood's Spanish accent, calling it "terrible," after the initial distraction of hearing it come out of a Northern California-born known luminary of Russian ancestry, it was easy to settle into her performance and realize that she was doing most everything precisely right. Her Maria was touching, resilient, properly naïve, and convincingly angry when required. As this role came so soon on the heels of another of her best performances, as the high school girl driven to a breakdown by puritanical guilt in *Splendor in the Grass*, Wood could count 1961 as one of her career peaks, giving her absolute best, which this time was very good indeed. Over time, *West Side Story* would be the movie for which most people would know her; it was to her credit that she had so wonderfully risen to the occasion, dubbed singing voice or not.

For Rita Moreno this was her long overdue moment in the critical spotlight. Authoritative from her first moment onscreen, she was spot-on with her reading of each line and created little doubt in anyone's mind that she had been the only real choice to essay the character of Anita. While she was the first to admit that she could never compete with a dancer as adept as Chita Rivera, she contributed thrillingly to both the "Dance at the Gym" and "America" numbers, and audiences responded to her as if a brand-new talent had suddenly, belatedly risen to the surface. It was not just an acclaimed performance but the sort that had "award consideration" stamped all over it. It seemed not to matter at all that she had had one of her key moments, the singing of "A Boy Like That," snatched away and given to another to interpret against her wishes. As such now-prominent accolades as the National Society of Film Critics had not yet been established and the New York Film Critics did not create a category for Supporting Actress until 1969, it is hard to determine how she might have fared in certain circles. Her first recognition would come with a Golden Globe nomination from the Hollywood Foreign Press, which she went on to win.

Also winning that honor was George Chakiris, who certainly was treated like the "next big deal" in Hollywood, his under-the-radar career as a backup dancer having given him no prior opportunities to shine front and center. Chakiris was sexy, dangerous, and, having been a basically silent commodity in the past, sounded authentically Hispanic to those unaware of his Ohio roots (Moreno's opinion on *his* accent is undocumented). His dance moves were dazzlingly smooth, he had charm, and he put in a very good performance to boot. Inasmuch as Wood, Beymer, and Tamblyn had already entered the fan consciousness through movie magazines and press releases, and Moreno was on the brink of turning thirty, Chakiris was the chief beneficiary of the huge attention *West Side Story* received, and the publicity machines went into overdrive playing up a newfound star.

Certainly it did not hurt to hear words like "masterpiece" being bandied about, but New York audiences were hyped to see the movie regardless; its opening week run at the Rivoli was nothing less than a smash, with capacity houses reported in *Variety* for every single show. Certainly many a big-screen musical had enjoyed a healthy audience response up front in recent years, but this time the crowds had a little something more to get excited about. In the previous year films like the adaptation of Cole Porter's *Can-Can*, the Franz Liszt biopic *Song Without End*, and the all-star *Pepe* had done quite nicely upon opening in Manhattan. Each of them, however, represented so much that was no longer "modern" and fresh about too many movie musicals. *Can-Can*, despite the presence of Frank Sinatra and Maurice Chevalier, was stilted and charmless; *Song Without End* was the sort of classical composer fantasy that might have appeared moldy and cornball in the prewar years; *Pepe* had the antiquated feeling of one of those star-stuffed offerings from the early talkies or the war years, meant to dazzle audiences with glimpses of luminaries coyly acknowledging their own fame. *West Side Story,* while carrying on certain conventions of the genre, seemed alive and original, technologically state-of-the-art and socially relevant to the times. Unlike so many others before it that seemed to care about pleasing traditionalists, this musical had the ability to appeal to both the old and the young. It was Broadway show music at its best, but the youthful slant of its story line made it very desirable for teens as well. Awed by the movie's increasing and continuing success, United Artists Executive Vice President Arnold M. Picker credited the vast interest to "Story, choreography, emergence of the younger generation, the oldest story in the world brought up to date."

As was the custom with a road-show engagement roll-out, *West Side Story* opened slowly at some of the major cities throughout the United States, next up being Boston at the 1,277-seat Gary in early November, followed later that month by Philadelphia's 1,000-plus-seat Midtown Theatre (later renamed the Prince Music Theater, after one of *West Side Story*'s original producers, Harold Prince), for what would evolve into a year-long run, and the Uptown in Washington, D.C., where it attracted crowds for the next nine months. (That theater's follow-up attractions were the Cinerama features *The Wonderful World of the Brothers Grimm* and *How the West Was Won*, which meant that for more than two years running this venue exclusively showed movies featuring Russ Tamblyn in the cast.) Since the film was required to open in the Los Angeles area in order to qualify for Academy Awards, it finally made its bow there on December 13, 1961, at the fabled 1,408-seat Chinese Theatre on Hollywood Boulevard, where the picture's star, Natalie Wood, had just placed her handprints in the forecourt earlier that month. That same week the picture premiered at the United Artists Theatre in San Francisco. Proving that the work was not simply a New York phenomenon, the incredible box office response was repeated from city to city as the movie played to packed houses in each venue.

The word was spreading fast that the film was something special to see, so another batch of reserved-seat openings followed in February 1962, bringing the picture to the Nixon in Pittsburgh; the Ohio in Cleveland; the 1,000-seat Mann in Minneapolis; the Madison in Detroit; the Mayfair in Baltimore; and finally to Chicago, at the 1,089-seat Michael Todd Theater. By the month's end *West Side Story* had its prestigious overseas debut, as the chosen offering for the sixteenth Annual Royal Film Performance for Queen Elizabeth I and Princess Margaret at the Odeon Leicester Square. Robert Wise, Russ Tamblyn, Richard Beymer, and George Chakiris were among those in attendance. The actual reserved-seat run of the film, however, would take place at the Astoria Theatre on Charing Cross Road, which had the largest advance sale in its history—yet another testament to *West Side Story*'s ability to transcend its very American identity. And the universal reach went beyond London, where the property had fared so well onstage.

A March 21 ad in *Variety* gave a rundown of the worldwide response (all prints of the film being subtitled, not dubbed): at Tokyo's Piccadilly Theatre it quickly became the all-time top grosser in less than a month's time; Stockholm's Ritz boasted of having been sold out months in advance;

Brussel's Ambassador claimed every performance a complete sell-out; Amsterdam's DuMidi Theatre had "advance sale building to new heights"; and the George V Theatre in Paris was turning away crowds at every performance. Indeed, the last country was worth noting, as the French had a reputation for reacting to Hollywood musicals with a collective shrug. This, however, was certainly not the case with *West Side Story*, which became such a phenomenon that this particular venue would show it continuously for a four-year stretch!

Back in the States, the place that had premiered the film, Manhattan's Rivoli, was adding matinees, and further bookings were taking place in Buffalo's Teck Theater, Cincinnati's Valley Theater, and Kansas City's Plaza. Despite the fact that it was still something ticket buyers had to go out of their way to see, *West Side Story* could claim by late March 1962 to be the number 1 box office attraction nationwide. By that point the ads could boast that the picture had garnered eleven Academy Award nominations.

The Oscars

When the Academy of Motion Picture Arts and Sciences announced their nominations on February 26, 1962, *West Side Story* was already being talked up as the front-runner in the race. The film was cited in nearly all categories in which it was eligible. It addition to Best Picture (where Robert Wise was the sole nominee as the official producer), it picked up mentions for director, thereby giving the Academy its first joint nomination, for Wise and Robbins; screenplay adaptation for Ernest Lehman; art direction, cinematography, costumes, film editing, music scoring, and sound; plus supporting acting citations for Rita Moreno and George Chakiris. The eleven nominations were a sure sign that *West Side Story* was highly admired by the Academy, although it was not the record holder in the race. There was competition in Stanley Kramer's bold, star-laden examination of the post–World War II trials, *Judgment at Nuremberg*, which had been a major attraction since its December 1961 opening and earned eleven nods as well. The other three films up for the Best Picture trophy were another formidable performer at the box office, the adventure epic *The Guns of Navarone*; the "small" and bleak critics' favorite, *The Hustler*; and the weakest of the bunch, the audience-friendly adaptation of *Fanny*, which was going into the contest without a nomination in the director category, usually a sign that a nominated film did not stand a chance.

Because the visual awards were still split into color and black-and-white nominations at this point in Academy history, *West Side Story*'s director of photography, Daniel L. Fapp, was also in the running that year for *One Two Three*, although that picture's monochromatic process meant he was not going up against himself. Costume designer Irene Sharaff, however, was filling two slots in the same (color) category, her creations for Universal's opulent adaptation of Rodgers and Hammerstein's *Flower Drum Song* bringing her the other mention. Likewise, Gordon Sawyer was in the running for the sound design on both *West Side Story* and *The Children's Hour*.

Rita Moreno stood a pretty good chance as the victor unless Academy voters felt it was time to honor Judy Garland, who had impressed with her nonmusical performance in *Judgment* as an excitable German witness. Moreno was also up against previous supporting actress winner Fay Bainter in *The Children's Hour*; Lotte Lenya, who was basically credited with putting some zing into a year-end failure, *The Roman Spring of Mrs. Stone*; and Una Merkel, who had mainly spent her career in comedy and had gone serious for a picture that also wasn't much good, *Summer and Smoke*.

Less of a sure thing was George Chakiris, as he had to compete with Montgomery Clift, who had been scarily on the mark as an unhinged witness in *Judgment* and had never received a trophy from the Academy; two outstanding performers from *The Hustler*, George C. Scott in a mesmerizingly intimidating turn and Jackie Gleason, who was proving himself adept at drama; and Peter Falk, who had done a comical flipside in *Pocketful of Miracles* of the more serious kind of role for which he'd been nominated the year before, in *Murder, Inc.* If any of the men were to be given less consideration when the time came to vote, it would be Scott, who declared himself so unimpressed by the honor that he asked to have his name withdrawn and went on record as being the first actor to refuse his nomination.

While it's unlikely anybody had considered putting Richard Beymer in the Best Actor category, in light of his lack of critical support, there was a chance of Natalie Wood ending up in the leading actress slot. However, she did have a straight drama running in theaters that placed her more firmly in the spotlight without a lot of other elements around her pulling focus, *Splendor in the Grass*. As she did end up being cited for that movie, she would therefore be in attendance at that year's ceremony. *West Side Story* had no original songs written for the screen, nor was it the sort of picture to draw attention to its special effects; therefore those were the only technical categories in which its name would not be read. Otherwise, it was quite well represented by the Academy.

Hosted by then-Oscar perennial Bob Hope, the ceremony was held at the Santa Monica Civic Auditorium on April 9, 1962. If there was doubt in anybody's mind that the dancingest movie in town might come out the top prize winner, they had only to consider the Academy's choice to present the Best

Picture award—the man who epitomized dance on film, Fred Astaire. Perhaps as a mea culpa for being uncharitably booted off his own picture, the Academy had voted to bestow a special Oscar upon Jerome Robbins. This was certainly justified in terms of his particular accomplishment on *West Side Story* but seemed curious otherwise, inasmuch as Robbins was first and foremost a figure of live theater, not motion pictures. If Hollywood was hoping this accolade would convince him to stick around and keep expanding his talents on the big screen, the gesture was in vain. Robbins would never again be involved in the world of film. Fittingly, this particular award would be given that night by the *other* great name in cinematic footwork, Gene Kelly. (There was no recorded statement on how Robbins felt about being handed the Oscar by someone who had scrapped his choreography and created his own dances for the film of *On the Town*.)

There was a clear feeling that evening of *West Side* dominance, as the first award given, for documentary, was presented by George Chakiris (along with Carolyn Jones). Next up, Irene Sharaff was named the winner for costume design—color, not for her showier designs from *Flower Drum Song* but for the simpler, more casual wear from *West Side Story*. Although the Academy had often awarded the trophy in this category for period pictures and opulence, this indicated that the movie did everything so very right that the industry was going to pay tribute to it in every way possible. This was even more evident when the year's previous supporting actress recipient, Shirley Jones, announced the winner for Best Supporting Actor, George Chakiris (the only one of his competition in attendance was Peter Falk), who was clearly flabbergasted by the victory.

And the title *West Side Story* kept being read by the evening's presenters, category after category, with film editing, scoring of a musical, and sound followed shortly thereafter by Robbins' special honor. Indeed, it was only in the categories in which it was *not* nominated that the film was not emerging triumphant. When Rock Hudson (standing in for Peter Ustinov) presented Rita Moreno with the Oscar for Best Supporting Actress, she no longer had to feel shown up by her date, having attended the ceremony on the arm of costar George Chakiris. Wins for cinematography and art direction made it clear that all other contenders might as well tear up their acceptance speeches. Only when Jack Lemmon and Lee Remick appeared onstage to present the writing awards was the *West Side Story* winning streak finally broken, with the adapted screenplay prize going to Abby Mann for *Judgment at Nuremberg*. (Ernest Lehman was not just the only nominee from *West Side Story* not to win that night, but he would *never* win a competitive Oscar. He was compensated with a special trophy in 2001.)

Chosen to give the Best Director award was Rosalind Russell, who had never worked with Robert Wise but actually had a Jerome Robbins connection, having starred in *Wonderful Town* on Broadway, on which he had served as an uncredited play "doctor," tweaking the troubled production out of town. The win by Wise and Robbins marked a milestone in the history of the Academy, this being the first time two people were honored together in the directorial category (the next time it happened was in 2007, when Joel and Ethan Coen won for *No Country for Old Men*). Many noted that despite the faces they had put on for the press, making it seem as if all was harmoniously settled over finishing the picture together, Wise and Robbins were not the closest of collaborators; neither man thanked the other during his acceptance speech. (There was also no "victory by proxy" for Natalie Wood, as she lost the Best Actress award for *Splendor in the Grass* to an absent Sophia Loren.) By the time Fred Astaire arrived onstage (past the two-hour mark, the first time the telecast went over that cutoff point), it certainly would have been curious indeed had *Fanny* been read upon opening the envelope. As it stood, that particular movie had garnered nothing all evening, while *The Guns of Navarone* won one award and *The Hustler* and *Judgment at Nuremberg* won two apiece. The Best Picture win for *West Side Story* put its total at ten, excluding Robbins' honorary award. There were few ready to argue with the choice. The picture was already being spoken of as a modern classic.

As was apt to happen to any Best Picture Oscar winner, the box office surged after the ceremony, as *West Side Story* stayed the number 1 attraction in America, expanding its hold over the next several months at such venues as the Elmwood in Providence; the Admiral in Omaha; the Lyric in Indianapolis; the Denham in Denver, the Hiland in Albuquerque, and the Brown in Louisville. In the New York metropolitan area, the same week of the Oscar win, 70 mm prints of the film began playing at the St. James in Asbury Park, New Jersey; the Syosset on Long Island; and the Bellevue in Upper Montclair, New Jersey. April, May, and June 1962 found it holding its spot at the top of the box office charts. The movie was turning into the sort of money-making phenomenon of which every distributor dreams.

On Record

Columbia Records' original soundtrack album of the film was released to coincide with *West Side Story*'s October 1961 unveiling. The single-disc recording was first issued in what was called a gatefold, allowing the buyer to open up the cover, whereupon there was an extensive essay on the making of the film, along with plot description and still photos. In order to fit everything on one LP, the overture and end title music were eliminated. No mention was made in the packaging of the dubbing contributions of Marni Nixon, Jimmy Bryant, or Betty Wand; indeed, with the song titles that appeared inside the gatefold, *nobody* was credited for singing.

Days after the movie opened at the Rivoli in Manhattan, the October 23, 1961, issue of *Billboard*, the show business weekly that covered the music industry, reported the soundtrack as having entered the Top 200 Best Selling Album charts at a very unimpressive number 128. It hardly mattered, for it quickly jumped to the number 81 spot the next week and then number 58 the following, not a bad showing for a soundtrack of a film that was only available in New York at that point. On November 13, the album really began its swift ascent, being tracked (as was the norm at the time) for both its Stereophonic and Monaural sales, landing at number 45 on the former chart, number 48 on the latter. This was not the era in which rock 'n' roll was dominating the LP charts, although it was a constant presence in the singles listings. At the time the *West Side Story* soundtrack debuted, the top of the charts listed such artists as Judy Garland, Johnny Mathis, the Broadway cast album of *Camelot*, and Elvis' soundtrack for *Blue Hawaii*. The songs from *West Side Story* fit very comfortably into this era, being "easy listening" for adult buyers yet sounding "hip" enough for the teens. By early December the LP had cracked the

Stereo Top 20, hitting number 9 there on January 6, 1962. The Monaural was slower in its climb, as the stereo was clearly the preferred album.

The soundtrack, however, was not the *only* album to reflect the picture's increasing popularity. The movie's debut had a terrific impact on the 1957 original Broadway cast album, which re-emerged in the public eye, leaping in sales and returning to the *Billboard* charts. Likewise, two records that had jumped upon the impending interest in the motion picture charted as well: piano duo Ferrante and Teicher's *West Side Story* LP on United Artists Records and jazzman Stan Kenton and his group's take on the score on Capitol Records. Interestingly, both albums featured artwork taken directly from the movie: the former was adorned with a cluster of color photo highlights and the latter was sold with an image of Russ Tamblyn and the Jets dancing down the street. Ferrante and Teicher were responsible for the sole hit single recording to benefit from the movie's release at the time, their version of "Tonight" peaking at number 8 in November 1961.

Meanwhile, after a one-week dip to number 13, the *West Side Story* soundtrack returned to the Stereo Top 10 on January 27, 1962, where it would remain for an unprecedented ninety-three-week run, finally dropping to number 11 on November 9, 1963, only to bounce back up to number 9 the following week. On May 5, 1962, the soundtrack finally hit the number 1 position on the Monaural charts. The following week it managed to knock Henry Mancini's soundtrack for *Breakfast at Tiffany's* from the top of the Stereo rankings, thereby making May 12, 1962, the date that the *West Side Story* soundtrack secured the number 1 spot on both charts for the first time. It would stay there until June 23, when Ray Charles' *Modern Sounds in Country and Western Music* would knock it down to second place on the Mono chart. (Charles' LP contained the singer's longest charting number 1 single, "I Can't Stop Loving You.") During this time the Grammy Awards voted *West Side Story* the winner for Best Sound Track Album or Recording of an Original Cast from Motion Pictures or Television. *Kenton's West Side Story* LP was awarded Best Jazz Performance by a Large Group (Instrumental). The *West Side Story* cast album could also boast of having reached the number 5 spot on the Mono chart on June 16, 1962, nearly five years after its debut.

Monaurally, *West Side Story* managed to regain its top spot from Ray Charles in October, but the Stereo sales in no way abated during that time. From May 12, 1962, until March 9, 1963, *West Side Story* reigned supreme over the Stereo charts, only moving for a week when *Jazz Samba* by Stan Getz and Charlie Byrd dethroned it. In a blink the soundtrack was right back at number 1 the next week, where it stayed until June 1, 1963, when it was overtaken by Andy Williams' *Days of Wine and Roses*. Although it would never again peak so high, it stayed a mighty chart force well into 1964. (At the time *Meet the Beatles* hit number 1 on February 15, 1964, the *West Side Story* soundtrack was not far off, positioned at number 5.) It finally dipped out of the *Billboard* Top 40 on July 25, 1964, by which time it had already reached legendary status in the music industry for its endurance. There was no other record of any kind with such staying power during the 1960s. Indeed, it would remain the champ in number of weeks spent on the music charts, holding the number 1 position longer than any other soundtrack album or album of *any* kind in recording history. Not bad for a record on which so many buyers weren't even aware of just *who* they were listening to.

CHAPTER 4

Afterstory

Tonight . . . and Every Night

The theater where it all began, the Rivoli, played host to *West Side Story* for an incredible 77-week run, finally vacating the spot in April 1963 for Marlon Brando's *The Ugly American*. At the time the only movie that had played in the same road show house longer was *Around the World in Eighty Days* (1956), which had been at that location for two years. On the first anniversary of the *West Side Story*'s October 18 opening, *Variety* reported that it had earned $8,341,362 in its 326 U.S. engagements, approximately $21,000,000 worldwide, and $1,987,000 at the Rivoli alone. This was prior to its going into general release (or "at popular prices," as the expression went). There was no denying that *West Side Story* had become a sensation, one of the touchstone pieces of pop culture that defined the early 1960s, despite its origins in the end of the previous decade. By the time it was officially finished with its initial run, it had reached the number 5 position on *Variety*'s chart of the biggest moneymaking motion pictures of all time, with rentals of $19 million, or approximately a $40 million gross, following *Gone with the Wind, Ben-Hur, The Ten Commandments,* and *Around the World in Eighty Days.*

Having clearly excited the nation into reconsidering what many of them might have missed live, *West Side Story* was staged in Los Angeles at Frank Sennes' Moulin Rouge on Sunset Boulevard in 1962 by the film's Action, Tony Mordente. Mordente's then-wife, Chita Rivera, reprised her role of Anita from the original production, and Larry Kert was back playing Tony. Also from the movie's cast were Tucker Smith, David Winters, Gus Trikonis, and Andre Tayir. Two years later the musical returned to New York, albeit for a limited run of thirty-one performances at the City Center, starting in April 1964. Under the direction of Gerald Freedman, with Jerome Robbins' choreography remounted by the film's Gee-Tar, Tommy Abbott, the new production would be just one of many to forever divide those who felt that the excitement of seeing it in person was never going to be duplicated in a motion picture, no matter how acclaimed, and those who had been so thoroughly enthralled by how the story was presented for cinema that the stage seemed to hinder and restrict it. This version included from the film Jay Norman (now promoted to playing Bernardo) and Eliot Feld, fighting for the rival side, cast as a Shark. In June 1968 the musical was back again for New York audiences, this time at the State Theater at Lincoln Center, which meant it was playing approximately on the spot where the opening of the film had been shot. It ran for eighty-three performances, with Lee Theodore reproducing the Robbins staging.

That same year, United Artists decided to see if 1968 audiences would respond as eagerly as had moviegoers a mere seven years earlier. The times, after all, had changed considerably in that seemingly short gap, and there was less chance of "show music" dominating the record charts, while a newer degree of permissiveness was entering moviemaking in ways that were already making films from the first half of the decade come off as old-fashioned. *West Side Story*, however, had seemed so vibrantly current and alive in style and content that its message was never more potent, the cinematic artistry with which it was accomplished never more stunning. In the wake of youthful unrest, campus uprisings, and the increasing "generation gap," a movie about pure love destroyed by societal and racial pressures couldn't have seemed more in tune. (At the time the definitive motion picture version of *Romeo and Juliet*, directed by Franco Zeffirelli, was creating a stir.) United Artists made sure to emphasize the youth aspect with the unforgettable tag line, "Unlike most movies, *West Side Story* grows younger." Re-released at area theaters on November 20, 1968, the film managed another impressive run that justified the decision to bring it back to the big screen, where it most certainly belonged.

Television, however, was anxious to have it and had been dangling offers to UA for the home premiere showing, actually closing a deal in 1967 with NBC prior to the theatrical reissue. The network paid approximately $5 million for the rights, part of a package deal with the distributor. Viewers, however, would have to wait another five years for their chance to see it on the small screen, and when that moment arrived NBC could not have done the movie a more grave injustice. Not only were the Wise-Robbins compositions insensitively ignored by the common television tradition of reframing wide-screen theatrical features to fit a square space, but somebody made the curious decision to cut the picture in half to air in two 90-minute increments over a two-night stretch, March 14 and 15, 1972. This blatantly disregarded Wise's original intention to eliminate the intermission altogether to keep the tension of the story line building. Therefore *West Side Story* debuted in a visibly reduced format, riddled with commercials, and with beginning and conclusion separated by a day. Yet still there was a huge interest, as a new generation watched unfold a picture that most defiantly did not seem like anything else being offered on the *NBC Saturday/Monday/Tuesday . . . Night at the Movies*. Whether viewers found it enthralling, dynamic, odd, corny, or whatever, there was no getting around the fact that *West Side Story*, even in a truncated version, still produced a palpable reaction. It was indelible, it had a strong hold on the public, it was not something easily dismissed. It was a magnificent, mighty achievement no matter how one looked at it, and it would not slip into the past as would other musicals, both onstage and onscreen, from the same era. It continued to play on both prime time and syndicated television for decades, winning new fans who discovered and were excited by just how good the material was. Those more adventurous than the people who considered television the be-all and end-all of a motion picture's lifespan tracked it down in its occasional returns to the big screen, well aware that the experience would be enhanced thoroughly. In the meantime, it became a perennial on the home video market and could at last be enjoyed in something akin to the correct ratio when the laserdisc and then DVD formats came along. Viewers discovered the way the "Prologue," "Dance at the Gym," and "Cool" were *supposed* to be seen.

An interesting sidelight was the "novelization" that was released in conjunction with the picture's theatrical run by

Cardinal Press in November 1961. Written by Irving Shulman (hired, no doubt, because he'd authored one of the earlier novels on gang violence, *The Amboy Dukes,* and worked on the definitive troubled teen picture of the fifties, *Rebel Without a Cause*), it is a curious tie-in to the musical, having, of course, no time for song and dance breaks, painting a more bleak portrait of urban decay, and attempting to explore the sociological origins of urban gangs in more detail. There are last names for the protagonists, Riff Lorton, Maria Nunez, Tony Wyzek, Anita Palacio, Chino Martin; some unfortunate cheap swipes at homosexuals (in light of the four creators of the original show being gay, this stands out especially), and such minor alterations as having the "war council" occur at a place called The Coffee Pot rather than Doc's. Most novelizations are quick to fade away, to be unearthed later in used book shops, but this one simply would not die. Once again reflecting the incredible degree of devotion people carried for the film, Shulman's take on *West Side Story* kept getting reprinted, year after year and became a staple in libraries and bookstores for decades, as if it was a legitimate original novel.

When lists were made citing important achievements in not only the musical genre but the history of film, few did not note *West Side Story*'s status as one of the great accomplishments. It became and stayed one of the few motion pictures labeled a "classic" with little argument in the film community. With great pride in her involvement, Rita Moreno would sum up the feelings of so many: "*West Side Story* has *never* been equaled, let alone surpassed, in terms of *great* musicals," she declared in the documentary *West Side Stories*.

The theatrical community, of course, was less charitable with its praise. The fact that the four men responsible for the original stage production, Jerome Robbins, Leonard Bernstein, Arthur Laurents, and Stephen Sondheim, never missed an opportunity to denigrate the motion picture did no go unnoticed by their followers, who were quick to support their claims. Those with little use for Hollywood and filmdom's "vulgar" insistence on prioritizing the box office over artistic integrity believed that the movie of *West Side Story* was just another such case. As far as theater enthusiasts were concerned, live was unbeatable, and one had only to see *West Side Story* done in person to prove them right. Unfortunately, this was hardly the case the two times the property was officially brought back to Broadway.

The first, under Robbins' own watchful eye, arrived at the Minskoff Theatre on February 14, 1980, only to be declared, pretty much across the board, "bland." Twenty-nine years later the show returned, at the Palace Theatre, this time with Laurents at the helm. Efforts to keep things "politically correct" by having chunks of dialogue and even many of Stephen

Sondheim's lyrics translated into Spanish did not play well with audiences, and the consensus was that something special was missing. Not surprisingly, there was great public interest initially in both productions, and it would be fair to say that some ticket buyers were hoping the motion picture they loved so much would be well served or perhaps even better onstage.

But comparing stage to screen hardly mattered anymore. *West Side Story* was a great piece of theater *and* a great piece of cinema. In both cases it was seldom considered less than a classic of the genre, one of a handful of musicals filled with songs that were instantly recognizable, not only by those who followed the art form but also by the average citizen. Certainly it was the high-water mark for nearly everyone connected with the motion picture.

The Aftermath

Curiously, *West Side Story* was not a stepping-stone to greater, equally great, or even acceptable things for so many of those involved.

NATALIE WOOD

There was one true, across-the-board movie star in the cast when production began on *West Side Story*, and Natalie Wood remained the most famous performer afterward as well. The year following its release, she ended up in the screen version of yet another Robbins–Laurents–Sondheim collaboration, *Gypsy*, this time singing her own numbers, as a powerhouse voice was not required for the role of Louise. So angry were many fans that Ethel Merman was not allowed to repeat her legendary performance as Rose that the film was callously dismissed. It was hardly an embarrassing adaptation of a revered work, as this negativity suggested; Wood's contribution was one of her better acting efforts.

She remained in top form for the urban drama-comedy *Love with the Proper Stranger* (1963), which brought her yet another Oscar nomination and contains perhaps her most assured work. There were big box office returns for the slapstick comedy *The Great Race* (1965) and one of the seminal permissive satires of the late sixties, *Bob & Carol & Ted & Alice* (1969), which kept her name prominent with the general public. By the 1970s, she was less visible in theatrical features, although she remained a star "name." The stunned reaction to her tragic drowning on November 29, 1981, near Catalina Island was proof of just how beloved she was by both her fellow actors and moviegoers, and how much she would be missed.

RICHARD BEYMER

Having played a leading role in one of the most widely attended motion pictures of the 1960s should have sent

Richard Beymer's star soaring, but he was saddled with forever being considered the weak link in *West Side Story*. Certainly, there was not much left to his career as a rising star following the picture's release. He himself felt out of his element in the three big roles he was given afterward, *Five Finger Exercise* (1962), *Hemingway's Adventures of a Young Man* (1962), and *The Stripper* (1963). Indeed, his reviews for the Hemingway picture were particularly damning, and his costar in the last, Joanne Woodward, saw his strain in trying to keep up with the more assured cast members and suggested he study his craft back in New York. About the only pleasure Beymer found in his movie career was acting opposite Richard Burton in the all-star World War II epic *The Longest Day* (1962), which turned out to be yet another tremendous box office success with which he was associated.

Studying at the Actors Studio in Manhattan was not a revelatory experience for Beymer, who felt even more out of place there than on the Hollywood soundstages. Instead he was certain the future held a career *behind* the cameras, after making his own documentary about the civil rights struggle in Mississippi, *A Regular Bouquet*, which led to another effort as a director, a short called *A Very Special Day*. Having fallen way off the A list by the close of the 1960s, he turned up in a drug-themed exploitation film that went under the titles *Scream Free* and *Free Grass*. The only reasons it warrants any mention are that it reunited him with fellow celluloid gang member Russ Tamblyn and that the leading lady was one degree removed from Natalie Wood: her younger sister, Lana. During the 1970s, the only time Beymer had any connection with the world of movies was when he unleashed his nonlinear effort, *Innerview*, on the film festival market. In later years he admitted to having no idea exactly what the movie was about. Like it or not, he still had his connection to *West Side Story* to fall back on, and during the 1980s this began to pay off with filmmakers who had grown up on the picture and liked the idea of cashing in on Beymer's name. He resumed acting in the 1980s, albeit mostly in low-budget melodramas and direct-to-video fare. His one high-profile credit was David Lynch's cult-wannabe television series *Twin Peaks*, which also featured Tamblyn.

RUSS TAMBLYN

Directly after the release of *West Side Story*, Russ Tamblyn's movie career seemed to be continuing on an even keel. He was featured among the vast casts of both of MGM's much-heralded Cinerama story movies, *The Wonderful World of the Brothers Grimm* (dancing a bit, with Yvette Mimieux) and *How the West Was Won*, as a Civil War deserter. He was also the only *West Side Story* cast principal asked back by Robert Wise for another collaboration, *The Haunting* (1963), which earned a reputation as one of the best and most literate of all cinematic ghost stories. But his interest in acting began to wane as he decided he might want to dabble in art instead, turning down roles that included the lead in what would become one of television's syndication staples, *Gilligan's Island*, among others. When he did work it was in such nonsense as the campy Japanese monster adventure *War of the Gargantuas*, which only went to prove that the drop from the top was swift in the movie industry. Equally shoddy credits included such drive-in trash as *The Female Bunch, Dracula vs. Frankenstein*, and the unpleasant and inept *Satan's Sadists* (advertised as "Russ Tamblyn in his greatest role since *West Side Story*," which showed that even exploitation filmmakers had no qualms about reaching out to musical fans, so important was *West Side Story* in the pop culture consciousness). As the years rolled by Tamblyn simply couldn't seem to raise himself out of the *über*-fringes of motion pictures, but as Beymer had found, it worked wonders having been part of something as iconic as *West Side Story*: this seemed to be the reason he was called for the jobs he did get. *Twin Peaks* put him in the spotlight for a brief run, but once that series ended he was back to basics until he received a boost in the 2000s because of a familial connection: his daughter Amber landed her own television series, *Joan of Arcadia*, on which her dad appeared from time to time.

In the 1995 documentary *West Side Stories,* Tamblyn, no doubt reeling from years of projects that had no lasting impact of any kind, more than appreciated his connection with one of the musical genre's peaks. "If someone had come up to me at that time and said 'You better appreciate this, because this'll probably be the highest time in your life . . . you'll probably never top this' . . . and, you know, unless something miraculous happens, it's quite true. I'm sure I'll go to my grave and people will say 'Russ Tamblyn from *West Side Story*.'"

RITA MORENO

There would not have been much to say about Rita Moreno's direct follow-up film to *West Side Story* had it not been for the fact that *Cry of Battle* ended up a trivia question for conspiracy buffs because it was one of the two films playing (*War Is Hell* was the other) at the Texas Theatre in Dallas on November 22, 1963, when President Kennedy's alleged assassin, Lee Harvey Oswald, was captured there by the law. Curiously, despite her status as a new Oscar-winning actress, another six years would pass before movie audiences saw Moreno onscreen again, although few were present for the unveiling of *The Night of the Following Day*, starring a man with whom the actress had been attached to socially offscreen for a while, Marlon Brando. After this dry spell

Moreno once again became a steady, working actress on screen, stage, and television and made much of becoming one of the few show business personalities to win the "Big Four" awards, the Oscar, the Tony (for *The Ritz*), the Emmy (for guest appearances on *The Muppet Show* and *The Rockford Files*), and a Grammy (for performing on the soundtrack of the television show *The Electric Company*). She was *not*, however, this first person to achieve this, as she often erroneously stated: Helen Hayes had beaten her to the punch only months before. Moreno's film work included showing up to pleasure Jack Nicholson at the end of *Carnal Knowledge*, repeating her Broadway role of talentless bathhouse entertainer Googie Gomez in the adaptation of *The Ritz*, and using her Italian ancestry like a crutch in the comedy hit *The Four Seasons*. On television she was a regular on several series that failed to take off, including *Nine to Five, The Cosby Mysteries*, and *Cane*, and one that did, *Oz*, as a prison nun.

GEORGE CHAKIRIS

Receiving the big "fan magazine push" in light of his *West Side Story* success, George Chakiris kept very busy in films over the next three years, including two he did as part of his contract with the Mirisch Company, *Kings of the Sun*, an unpopular Mayan epic in which he was upstaged by Yul Brynner, and *633 Squadron*, where he was killed off early in the story. There seemed to be a pattern, for despite his award-worthy status he wasn't ever asked to carry a movie on his name alone. His biggest post–*West Side Story* money-earner, the soap opera *Diamond Head*, featured him in support of Charlton Heston and Yvette Mimieux, as the latter's defiantly angry half-caste lover.

Chakiris also got a recording "career" out of his involvement with *the* big musical of its era, putting out a series of albums for Capitol Records, including the self-titled *George Chakiris*, where he was billed on the jacket as "*West Side Story*'s Dynamic . . ." and which featured his own renditions of "Tonight" and "Maria." More interesting, visually, was the 1962 LP he did for the Horizon label, *The Gershwin Songbook*, as the album cover featured the actor stretched out on the floor, proudly grinning behind his Academy Award.

The heat began to cool in a very short time, so that there wasn't even much made of the fact that he returned to musicals by the decade's end, albeit overseas, in Jacques Demy's giddily artificial *The Young Girls of Rochefort*. Paired up with Grover Dale, he once again showed that his skills in this field were quite impressive, so smooth and graceful were his moves. Alas, by 1969 he was reduced to junk like the ridiculous Lana Turner LSD melodrama *The Big Cube*, by which point it was evident that he did not have that extra-special "something" that could override bad material. Like

Beymer and Tamblyn, he seldom again scaled A-list heights, although he kept acting, on stage (playing Bobby in a tour of *Company* and the Count in the West End's production of *The Passion of Dracula*, among others), on television (as Frederic Chopin in *Notorious Woman* on PBS and in a recurring role for one season of the long-running nighttime soap *Dallas*), and in scattered forays onto the big screen, although few pictures he did actually received theatrical distribution. Finally leaving the profession behind in the late 1990s, he turned to designing jewelry.

ROBERT WISE

While *West Side Story* was still packing theaters, Robert Wise's follow-up effort for the Mirisch Company, an adaptation of the two-character Broadway success *Two for the Seesaw*, opened to tepid reviews and slim box office returns. He fared better with the classy ghost story *The Haunting* in 1963, then returned to the top in a major way when he agreed to helm Twentieth Century-Fox's lavish production of Rodgers and Hammerstein's final Broadway musical, *The Sound of Music*. Many had been scared off by the potentially sticky nature of this property, but Wise took the challenge along with his *West Side Story* writer, Ernest Lehman, and managed to spin gold, coming up with an even bigger moneymaker than his previous foray into the field. What's more, the dexterity with which Wise managed to make this true story about nuns, children, and Nazis blend flawlessly into a hugely enjoyable and deeply moving commercial entertainment proved that it was not *all* Robbins' efforts that had made *West Side Story* click so well. *Music* not only topped *West Side Story* tenfold at the box office but also became *the* highest grossing film in history. It won the Academy Award for Best Picture and Wise took home another trophy as director.

Wise directed another winner for Fox the following year, the antiwar adventure *The Sand Pebbles* (1966), and although its many Oscar nominations did not include one for his direction, he was given the Irving G. Thalberg Award at that same year's ceremony, for his producing career. Since he'd been responsible for *the* blockbuster of the decade, the same studio, Fox, had no objections to Wise directing that same film's star, Julie Andrews, in a no-expense-spared biopic of Gertrude Lawrence. *Star!*, however, became one of those unfortunate old-fashioned musicals of the late 1960s that was deemed "out of touch" and wound up losing a small fortune. His next picture, the thinking man's sci-fi thriller *The Andromeda Strain*, did better business, thereby helping to wipe away the onus of failure within the industry. However, few of his 1970s efforts would rank among his best work. There was the speculative revision of one of history's tragic events, *The Hindenburg*, the supernatural *Audrey Rose*, and *Star Trek—The Motion Picture*, the sort of huge grosser about which nobody had anything good to say. Mostly resting on past triumphs as he entered his old age, Wise still received much praise and reverence for having given the world two musicals that continued to win worshipful admirers. Thanks mainly to *West Side Story* and *The Sound of Music*, he was given the Lifetime Achievement Award from the Directors Guild in 1988 and the American Film Institute Award ten years later (Rita Moreno was among those in attendance). He died in Los Angeles on September 14, 2005, four days after his ninety-first birthday.

JEROME ROBBINS

Considering his unceremonious dismissal from the set of *West Side Story*, it came as no surprise that Jerome Robbins never returned to filmmaking, but his admirers were unprepared for his decision to turn his back on Broadway as well. Following acclaim for *Fiddler on the Roof* (winning directorial and choreography Tonys), he turned his attention completely to ballet. When he did bother to revisit Broadway it was for the indifferently received 1980 *West Side Story* revival. Certainly he fared better with his "greatest hits" celebration of his own work, *Jerome Robbins' Broadway*, in 1989, which reminded New York theater audiences what a creative talent had been missing from Broadway for too long. It brought him his final Tony for Best Director. He died at his home in New York on July 29, 1998. Even among those not the least bit interested in classical dance or ballet, his name remained familiar and brought a smile of recognition and admiration, due almost certainly to its inextricable link with *West Side Story*.

THE CREDITS

Producer: Robert Wise

Directors: Robert Wise and Jerome Robbins

Screenplay: Ernest Lehman

Associate Producer: Saul Chaplin

Choreographer: Jerome Robbins

Music: Leonard Bernstein

Lyrics: Stephen Sondheim

Book: Arthur Laurents

Based on the stage play produced by: Robert E. Griffith and Harold Prince

Play Conceived, Directed and Choreographed by: Jerome Robbins

Production Designer: Boris Leven

Music Conductor: Johnny Green

Director of Photography: Daniel L. Fapp, A.S.C.

Costume Designer: Irene Sharaff

Assistant Director: Robert E. Relyea

Dance Assistants: Tommy Abbott, Margaret Banks, Howard Jeffrey, Tony Mordente

Film Editor: Thomas Stanford

Music Editor: Richard Carruth

Photographic Effects: Linwood Dunn, A.S.C., Film Effects of Hollywood

Orchestrations: Sid Ramin and Irwin Kostal

Sound: Murray Spivack, Fred Lau, Vinton Vernon

Musical Assistant: Betty Walberg

Vocal Coach: Bobby Tucker

Production Manager: Allen W. Wood

Titles and Visual Consultants: Saul Bass and Associates

Production Artist: M. Zuberano

Set Decorator: Victor Gangelin

Property: Sam Gordon

Sound Editor: Gilbert D. Marchant

Assistant Editor: Marshall M. Borden

Script Supervisor: Stanley K. Scheuer

Second Assistant Director: Jerome M. Siegel

Makeup: Emile La Vigne, S.M.A.

Hairdresser: Alice Monte, C.H.S.

Wardrobe: Bertg Henrikson

Casting: Stalmaster-Lister Co.

Filmed in Panavision 70

Technicolor

155 minutes

A Robert Wise production

Presented by Mirisch Pictures, Inc. in association with Seven Arts Productions, Inc.

Released through United Artists

The Cast

Maria .... Natalie Wood

Tony .... Richard Beymer

Riff .... Russ Tamblyn

Anita .... Rita Moreno

Bernardo .... George Chakiris

THE JETS

Ice .... Tucker Smith

Action .... Tony Mordente

A-Rab .... David Winters

Baby John .... Eliot Feld

Snowboy .... Bert Michaels

Tiger .... David Bean

Joyboy .... Robert Banas

Big Deal . . . . Scooter Teague
Mouthpiece . . . . Harvey Hohnecker
Gee-Tar . . . . Tommy Abbott

THEIR GIRLS

Anybodys . . . . Sue Oakes
Graziella . . . . Gina Trikonis
Velma . . . . Carole D'Andrea

THE SHARKS

Chino . . . . Jose De Vega
Pepe . . . . Jay Norman
Indio . . . . Gus Trikonis
Juano . . . . Eddie Verso
Loco . . . . Jaime Rogers
Rocco . . . . Larry Roquemore
Luis . . . . Robert Thompson
Toro . . . . Nick Covacevich
Del Campo . . . . Rudy Del Campo
Chile . . . . Andre Tayir

THEIR GIRLS

Consuelo . . . . Yvonne Othon
Rosalia . . . . Suzie Kaye

Francisca .... Joanne Miya

THE ADULTS

Lieutenant Schrank .... Simon Oakland
Officer Krupke .... William Bramley
Doc .... Ned Glass
Glad Hand .... John Astin
Madam Lucia .... Penny Santon

The Songs

Overture
"Prologue" .... danced by the Jets and the Sharks
"The Jet Song" .... Riff and the Jets
"Something's Coming" .... Tony
"Dance at the Gym" .... danced by the Jets and Their Girls, the Sharks and Their Girls
"Maria" .... Tony
"America" .... Anita, Bernardo, the Sharks, Their Girls
"Tonight" .... Maria, Tony
"Gee, Officer Krupke" .... Riff and the Jets
"I Feel Pretty" .... Maria, Consuelo, Rosalia
"One Hand, One Heart" .... Tony, Maria
"Quintet" .... the Jets, the Sharks, Anita, Tony, Maria
"The Rumble" .... the Jets and the Sharks

"Rooftop Dance" . . . . Maria
"Somewhere" . . . . Tony, Maria
"Cool" . . . . Ice, the Jets, Their Girls
"A Boy Like That/I Have a Love" . . . . Anita, Maria

THE SINGING VOICES

Maria . . . . Marni Nixon
Tony . . . . Jimmy Bryant
Riff (on "The Jet Song") . . . . Tucker Smith
Anita (on "A Boy Like That") . . . . Betty Wand
Anita (on "Quintet") . . . . Marni Nixon

BIBLIOGRAPHY

Books

Finstad, Suzanne. *Natasha: The Biography of Natalie Wood.* New York: Three Rivers Press, 2001.

Keenan, Richard C. *The Films of Robert Wise*. Lanham, MD: Scarecrow Press, 2007.

Laurent, Arthur. *Original Story By*. New York: Knopf, 2000.

Mirisch, Walter. *I Thought We Were Making Movies, Not History*. Madison: University of Wisconsin Press, 2008.

Nixon, Marni, with Stephen Cole. *I Could Have Sung All Night: My Story*. New York: Billboard Books, 2007.

Peyser, Joan. *Bernstein: A Biography*. New York: Beech Tree Books, 1987.

Secrest, Meryle. *Stephen Sondheim: A Life*. New York: Delta, 1999.

Shulman, Irving. *West Side Story: A Novelization of the Broadway Musical "West Side Story."* New York: Cardinal, 1961.

Articles

Archer, Eugene. "*West Side* Direction." *New York Times*, Oct. 15, 1961, 7.

Atkinson, Brooks. "West Side, Moving Music Drama on Callous Theme." *New York Times*, Oct. 6, 1957, 133.

Bart, Peter. "A Young Ex-Actor Returns to Films." *New York Times*, Sept. 9, 1964.

Becker, Bill. "Hollywood Steps." *New York Times*, July 3, 1960, 5.

Calta, Louis. "Two New Plays to Open Tonight." *New York Times*, May 16, 1957, 27.

———. "*West Side Story* to Be Told Again." *New York Times*, Jan. 13, 1960, 19.

Ciaccia, Maria. "Midwest Side Story: Richard Beymer." *Pathfinder: Where Are They Now*, 1997.

Crowther, Bosley. "Musical Advance." *New York Times*, Oct. 22, 1961, 1.

Funke, Lewes. "News and Gossip of the Rialto." *New York Times*, Jan. 22, 1956, 93.

———. "News and Gossip of the Rialto." *New York Times*, June 23, 1957, 89.

Gelb, Arthur. "Two More Musicals Offered Robbins." *New York Times*, Feb. 4, 1957, 15.

Gow, Gordon. "Take Off from Hollywood." *Films and Filming* (June 1975).

Johnson, Ian. "Russ Tamblyn: From Your First Cigarette to Your Last Dying Day." *Psychotronic* 8 (Winter 1990): 50–58.

Kaufman, George S. "Musical Comedy—or Musical Serious?" *New York Times*, Nov. 3, 1957, 223.

Masters, Dorothy. "A Honey Misses 'B' in Name of Beymer." *Sunday News*, Aug. 26, 1962, 6.

Nogueira, Rui. "Robert Wise to Date." *Focus on Film* (Autumn 1974).

Pryor, Thomas M. "*West Side Story* Sought for Film." *New York Times*, July 17, 1958, 31.

Rosenfield, Paul. "Richard Beymer Never Was a Soft Young Man." *Los Angeles Times*, Dec. 26, 1982, 27–28.

Rusk, Howard A. "The Facts Don't Rhyme." *New York Times*, Sept. 29, 1957, 83.

Schumach, Murray. "Talent Dragnet." *New York Times*, Sept. 22, 1957, 135.

Thompson, Howard. "At Work on *West Side Story*." *New York Times*, Aug. 14, 1960, 5.

INDEX